Pantheon
The Greeks

What People Are Saying About

Pantheon: The Greeks

A brilliant resource on Ancient Greek deities, mythology, and history. Irisanya Moon bridges the gap between devotional works, retellings of heroic epics, and academic studies. This book is packed with useful information aimed at modern pagans. It offers material to use in spiritual practice as well as being a concise reference book. *Pantheon: The Greeks* is also a delight to dip into purely for pleasure.
Lucya Starza, author of Pagan Portals titles *Candle Magic, Poppets and Magical Dolls, Guided Visualisations*, and *Scrying*, and the Gothic novel *Erosion*

What I have always admired about Irisanya Moon's work is that they don't shy away from the complexities of spirituality. In *Pantheon: The Greeks*, they convey the power, gifts, and shadow aspects of historic Greek worldview with scholarly and passionate detail. Through breaking down pivotal Greek texts to express the cultural and mythological ley, Moon demonstrates how these writings have been approached over time, and explores how they can come alive in spiritual practice now.
S. Kelley Harrell, author of *From Elder to Ancestor: Nature Kinship for All Seasons of Life*

Pantheon: The Greeks by Irisanya Moon is a wonderful guide to the Greek tradition and the Gods and beings that influenced not just the people of the time but have fascinated others from many cultures around the world right up until today. While the author has a scholarly approach to the subject, it is easy to follow and outlines the culture, customs, and celebrations that

influenced the tradition while giving an in-depth list of the Gods and beings, their symbolism, and their relation to one another, while relating the myths that bring them to life. Anyone who has an interest in the Greek tradition, I would recommend this book as a useful guide while walking the path, or as part of recommended reading on the subject.
Martha Gray, author of *Grimalkyn: The Witch's Cat: Power Animals in Traditional Magic*

For someone like me, who has loved the Greek myths since childhood, this book is perfect! Filled with myths, stories, analysis, timelines of Greek history, famous sites – everything you could possibly need to know about the Greek pantheon. I was particularly impressed with the scholarly nature of Irisanya's creation; and her ability to shed light on the often glossed over, difficult subjects, such as rape, in a methodical and objective manner. The writing style is accessible and engaging, making it suitable for everyone, whether a novice or seasoned connoisseur. Irisanya's deep devotion to everything Greek shines from every word of this book, which makes it a delightful read and cannot fail to inspire the reader to want to further their own studies. It is, in my opinion, the only guide you will need to help you develop a profound and meaningful relationship with the Greek deities.
Thea Prothero, author of *A Guide to Pilgrimage*

Pantheon
The Greeks

Irisanya Moon

London, UK
Washington, DC, USA

First published by Moon Books, 2025
Moon Books is an imprint of Collective Ink Ltd.,
Unit 11, Shepperton House, 89 Shepperton Road, London, N1 3DF
office@collectiveinkbooks.com
www.collectiveinkbooks.com
www.moon-books.net

For distributor details and how to order please visit the 'Ordering' section on our website.

Text copyright: Irisanya Moon 2024

ISBN: 978 1 80341 651 9
978 1 80341 650 2 (ebook)
Library of Congress Control Number: 2024942250

All rights reserved. Except for brief quotations in critical articles or reviews, no part of this book may be reproduced in any manner without prior written permission from the publishers.

The rights of Irisanya Moon as author have been asserted in accordance with the Copyright, Designs and Patents Act 1988.

A CIP catalogue record for this book is available from the British Library.

Design: Lapiz Digital Services

UK: Printed and bound by CPI Group (UK) Ltd, Croydon, CR0 4YY
Printed in North America by CPI GPS partners

We operate a distinctive and ethical publishing philosophy in all areas of our business, from our global network of authors to production and worldwide distribution.

Contents

Acknowledgments

I honor the land I live on, the unceded and colonized land of the Wappo, Coast Miwok, and Southern Pomo, also known as Santa Rosa, California, USA.

Thank you to my publisher, Moon Books / Collective Ink, for their unwavering support of my writing and magick. I have grown as a person and an author.

I have much gratitude for Trevor Greenfield and his support, kind words, silly jokes, and willingness to be patient with my ever-changing dedication to formatting guidelines.

Thank you to my friends and partner, who heard various drafts and complaints along the way. I appreciate your encouragement and willingness to listen to me hyperfixate on the writing process. And the editing process. So much editing.

I want to acknowledge my readers, the ones who reach out to me with kind words and stories about how my books have impacted their lives. I am honored to play the smallest part in your story.

And I thank the deities who continue to whisper in my ears and ask me to consider their fullness and complexity. These relationships have made me a better partner, friend, teacher, ritualist, writer, and human. The more I come to know the gods, the more I come to know myself and my own multi-faceted, sometimes petty, nature.

Author's Notes

Thank you for choosing this book and supporting my writing. I appreciate you, even if we never meet. Before you begin and certainly before you write a review, I encourage you to keep a few things in mind:

This is an introduction

This book is an introduction to the Greek pantheon. I hope it offers a strong foundation for readers and inspires you to learn and to keep learning, but...

Some details/practices/beings were left out

I could not include ALL the Greek beings or in the detail they likely deserve. I focus on the history and culture of ancient Greece, place the myths in context, summarize practices and beliefs, and describe the gods to help you better know them. Here, for example, are *some* beings not included or not included in detail: Agathos/Tychon, Ajax, Amazons, Amphitryon, Atalanta, Bellerophon, Cassandra, Cerus, Daedalus, Enyalios, Hecuba, Helen of Troy, Hermaphroditus/Hermaphroditos, Hymenaios, Icarus, Niobe, Morpheus, Nireus, Panacea, Penelope, and Sisyphus.

My use of 'Gods' vs. Gods and how I feel about pronouns

Readers of my books and other works will know that I use the spelling 'godds' to talk about deities, except when quotes from other authors use the more common spelling. My choice is meant to create a more gender-full experience of beings who I feel exist beyond the confines of gender. (Thanks to my beloved Urania for her initial use of 'godds.') I also don't believe gods have pronouns. That said, I use he/him and she/her when referring to different godds, based on how they have been described in the myths. However, I am CERTAIN Dionysus and Hermes, for example, would probably use 'they' pronouns.

However, in this book, as it is part of a series on different Pantheons written by different authors, I have agreed to revert to common practice and refer to gods, rather than godds.

Spellings vary

From one book to another, Greek deity and being names vary. These spellings are often based on the transliteration[1] of Greek words, as it helps to preserve the original language. Other spellings are based on Latin, and there are Roman versions of Greek deities (e.g., Venus vs. Aphrodite). Any mistakes or missteps in spelling and form are unintentional, as my ancient/modern Greek is a work in progress. For consistency, I decided to use these spellings for well-known gods, but I have included additional variations since you may find others in your ongoing study. I hope to avoid confusion as best I can.

Primordial Gods: Gaia, Nyx, Chronos, Eros, Oceanus, Thalassa, Ananke, Hemera, Ourea, Pontus, Tethys, Uranus

Titans: Coeus, Crius, Cronus, Hyperion, Iapetus, Mnemosyne, Oceanus, Phoebe, Rhea, Tethys, Theia, Themis

Olympian Gods: Aphrodite, Apollo, Ares, Artemis, Athena, Demeter, Dionysus, Hephaestus, Hera, Hermes, Hestia, Poseidon, Zeus

Underworld Gods: Hades, Persephone (Kore)

Reconstructionism is great, but not the focus

This book does not focus on Hellenism.[2] While I bring forward pieces of information about rituals and practices, I do not focus on how to recreate these on your own.

My modern practice will influence this writing and probably add bias

My practice with the Greek gods is modern and influenced by the practices, leaning into the stories for inspiration, but not beholden to them. (I have included many resources to help you find more details like this.)

I write about the Greeks from my perspective. As such, with no ill intent, I will likely have some bias in my writing. I've tried diligently to avoid this, and I'm human. I hope there are discussions about how I have presented the material, as I want to continue to learn and am committed to curiosity and ongoing learning.

I also include some of the stories of the gods because I believe in connecting on an emotional level, which, for me, happens through the evocation of feeling and connection – which is one of the many uses of myth.

If this book is the start of a spiritual journey, I encourage you to remain open to the gods and how they arrive for you. What works for me (or even for those in ancient Greece) might not work for you, and vice versa. After all, your relationship with the gods is YOUR relationship. May your journey be blessed.

Introduction

Unlike many, I was not introduced to Greek mythology in school. Maybe this is because I went to Catholic schools, or I missed the lesson when I moved to a new state.

I met the gods later, as references in pop culture, movies, and songs. I sought out information about deities when I started to practice witchcraft. I learned as I went along, acquainting myself with these gods as they appeared in myths, rituals, and Reclaiming classes.

Artemis and Gaia came early in my witch story, and later, Iris encouraged me to train in the Reclaiming Tradition. Hecate was loud from the start. Athena, Apollo, and Hestia found me in classes I taught and took. Aphrodite was later, I think, but I also believe she has been around for longer than I realized. Of course.

The Muses, the Fates, Dionysus, and Circe arrived in glimpses of art and story and song. They whispered in my ear and encouraged me to say what I felt and experienced.

My DNA will show my German, British, and Irish ancestry, and while I have worked with deities from those lands (and still do), my heart is with the Greeks. Even though I (and will continue to) make fun of them and their drama(s), I am deeply in love with the stories, characters, and complexity.

After numerous interactions with Greek gods, I have built long-term relationships, and I am honored to be able to share more about these deities that I call family. Sharing their stories (some of them, anyway) and sharing this magick is part of my service too.

When stories are told, magick stays alive.

[Iris speaks to Poseidon]
I came here bearing a message for you, dark-haired
holder of the earth, from Zeus who wields the aegis.
He commands you to desist from war and battle
and to go among the tribe of gods, or into the bright salt sea.
And if you do not obey his words, but ignore them,
he threatens that he too will come here
to do battle, face-to-face; and he bids you avoid
his hands, since he says he is more powerful by far than you in strength
and in birth is elder. Yet your own heart does not shrink
from deeming yourself his equal – he whom even the other god's dread.

The Iliad, Homer, Book 15, 174-183, translated by Caroline Alexander

My personal practice in the Greek pantheon began with the gods before I backtracked into history and Greek culture. Ideally, I would have built a better foundation, so I offer it to you. This book has two parts. Part I gives the background of ancient Greece. The sections will include:

- History
- Mythology
- Cosmology & Cosmogony
- Religion & Ritual
- Celebrations & Festivals
- Greek Magic
- Taking It Home

The goal for this first section is to allow you to settle into the environment where the gods, goddesses, and other beings show up. Like any good relationship, the more you can learn about context, the easier it is to find perspective and decide whether you are interested in learning more. We will explore rituals, celebrations, practices, and magic of the Greek pantheon, as much as we can ascertain from surviving information. This part will finish with thoughts about bringing these practices into your life.

Part II is dedicated to the gods and goddesses of the pantheon, as well as beings, creatures, monsters, and other important figures, their roles and relationships, tragedies, and power struggles. These beings make up a world that looks much like ours, and they continue to grace us (no pun intended) with their stories.

Part I

Chapter 1
History

Let's begin the history of the Greeks with this fact: there was and is no single group of Greeks. While books and articles speak of 'ancient Greece,' it is not a monolith, making it difficult to define or narrow it into a neat summary. The history is varied and involves numerous groups, interpretations, and translations of texts, settings, cultures, fragments of stories, etc.

> It is important to realize, when we talk of 'the Greeks of classical times' and 'classical Greece', that there was never a Greek nation in the sense that we speak today of, say, the French nation... The name 'Greeks' was not one which they themselves used. It is the Latin name for them, originally that of a small Greek tribe, with whom the people of Italy had early contact. The Greeks of classical times called themselves 'Hellenes' and their country 'Hellas' (as they still do today). The first Hellenes, too, were an obscure Greek tribe, whose name, by accidents of history, came to be applied to the whole race (Amos and Lang 4).

While I don't want to oversimplify history when it's complicated, I offer that the Greek story begins in a land where most citizens were within a day's walk of the Mediterranean Sea.[3] Most lived on farmland far from the rest of the world, with the sea serving as a route of connection and collaboration.

The land surrounding ancient Greece influences and inspires the stories. For example, Aphrodite was not from Greece but from Cyprus, an island to the east, and her image likely traveled by story from the place known today as Turkey, where temples to her image have been uncovered as recently as 2023.[4] Aphrodite's Rock, an area in Cyprus where she emerged from the water, is a place with ample sea foam, an important part of the story and relevant to her name, as ***aphros*** translates to 'foam.'

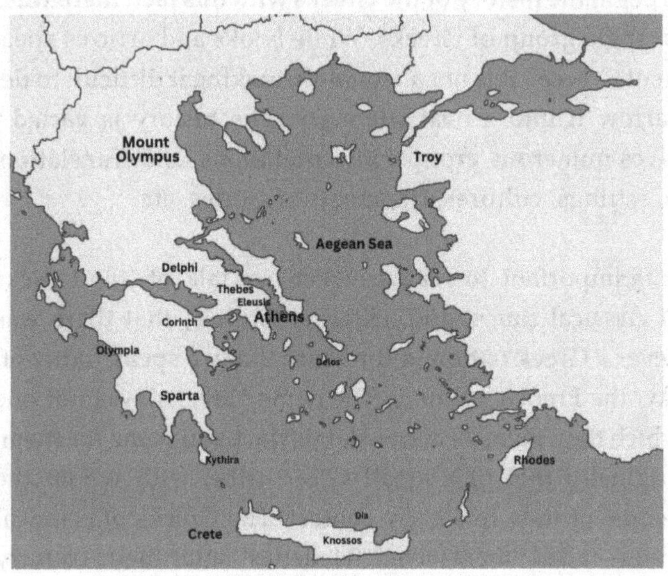

Map of Ancient Greece[5]

The weather was much the same as today: hot, dry summers across the coastal plains and hills. There were also forests of pine and barren areas. From Hesiod's *Works and Days*, as translated by Dorothea Wender, the land comes to life.

When the thistle blooms and on the tree
The loud cicada sits and pours his song
shrill and continuous, beneath his wings,
exhausting summertime has come. The goats
are very fat, the wine is very good.
Women are full of lust, but men are weak,

their heads and limbs drained dry by Sirius,
their skin parched from the heat. But at this time,
I love a shady rock, and Byblos wine,
a cake of cheese, and goat's milk, and some meat
of heifers pastured in the woods, uncalved,
or first-born kids. Then may I sit in the shade
And drink the shining wine, and eat my fill.

Let us remember the story of land, and what may be held in that wondrous geography. The land has held many stories and welcomed all that might be burdensome but also blooming. This land holds stories that continue to be sung and celebrated, questioned and retold, before all else, remember the land and the water and the brilliance and horror of man.

The History of Greece

> The diffusion of Greek culture throughout the Mediterranean area encouraged those Greeks who found themselves widely separated from their traditional homeland to define themselves conspicuously in terms of their shared culture. One prominent feature of this shared culture was the worship of a common pantheon of gods, headed by Olympian Zeus (Sansone 29).

People who spoke the Greek language, or the ancient Greeks, were a distinct group and civilization that lived in the eastern Mediterranean before 1000 BCE, or the Bronze Age.[6] The Linear B tablets (which will be detailed in a later chapter) were evidence of this language on the Greek mainland and Crete "from at least 1450 B.C.E. on the Greek mainland, although they almost certainly arrived in the area several hundreds of years before this" (Budin 3).

Greece's history[7] includes periods of growth, expansion, occupation, and modernity, including:

- Paleolithic Greece c. 3.3 million years ago to 20000 BCE
- Mesolithic Greece 13000 to 7000 BCE
- Neolithic Greece 7000 to c. 3100 BCE
- Bronze Age Greece c. 3200 to c. 1100 BCE
- **Ancient Greece 1200 BCE to c. 600 CE**
- Greek Dark Ages (Iron Age / Homeric Age) 1100 to 800 BCE
- Archaic Period 800 to 490 BCE
- Classical Period 490 to 323 BCE
- Hellenistic Period 323 to 146 BCE
- Roman Greece 146 BC to 324 CE
- Byzantine Greece 324 CE to 1453
- Frankish/Latin Greece 1204 CE to 1797
- Ottoman Greece 1453 CE to 1821
- Modern Greece 1821 to present

Ancient Greece is situated in a narrow period, and it is thought that Homer started to write down the stories in *The Odyssey* and *The Iliad* between the 8th and 7th century BCE. It's important to see the pattern of the Bronze Age before Ancient Greece and the Dark Ages. After times of growth and advancement, ancient Greece became defined (and documented) as a civilization.

The city-state (or ***polis***) emerged, offering a structure for building smaller towns and communities. The prominent city-states were Athens and Sparta. Democracy was an emerging thought in Athens, with the agreement that free men could attend government meetings and be a part of decision-making. This agreement hoped to take the power out of the hands of the aristocrats and put it back into the hands of the people. Because there were several coups and other power struggles during this time, this new system was expected to dissipate the issues, but it did not. The elites and the poor were still at odds, and democracy was not yet a fully formed practice. Like other countries, the expansion of voting rights is where democracy can be enacted most effectively, but women and persons of color don't gain their rights until later.

Sparta had two kings, a council of elders, and more power struggles. While conflicts continued, individual city-states started forming alliances, creating a more cohesive Greece. Sansone points out how the Greeks became aware of the idea of heroes from the ruins from the Mycenaean Period.[8] Because of evidence of funerary rites found around the eighth century, some people were celebrated at specific sites again and again. And while it is not clear if those who venerated the dead were descendants, it was clear they were important.[9]

What's also important to know about this time is that it was not only a period of the creation of Greece but also the beginning of Greece's influence over the Mediterranean region. Ancient Greece would give rise to new ideas about architecture, art, language, law, philosophy, poetry, politics, rhetoric, and more.

An ancient historian in the 5th century BCE, Thucydides, spoke of the region as 'settling down gradually' when today, Greece might be described as colonizing nearby lands to gain more power and influence.[10]

What Happened in Ancient Greece?

While there are many events in the space of ancient Greece, a few can be helpful in seeing what happened during the period of heroes and beyond.

1240 – The Trojan War starts and lasts 10 years
700s – Athens and Sparta begin
776 – The first Olympics happen in Olympia

750 – Homer writes *The Odyssey* and *The Iliad*
508 – The first democracy in Athens
490 – The Greeks win the Battle of Marathon to end the First Persian War
480 – The Greeks win the Battle of Salamis and the Second Persian War ends
404 – Sparta defeats Athens to end the Peloponnesian War
371 – Sparta is defeated by Athens and Thebes and other city-states
336 – Alexander the Great becomes king and conquers Persia, Egypt, and much of Asia
323 – Alexander the Great dies at the height of the Greek Empire
146 – The Roman Empire takes over Macedonia
86 – Athens is burned by Romans
30 – Greece becomes a part of the Roman Empire

While this is not comprehensive, it shows the movement of Greece from an emerging idea to a vast empire before succumbing to the Romans. These were wars and power struggles as groups tried to find their place in history after the introduction of deities and beings. Sansone notes:

> We have seen that Hesiod[11] inserted an age of heroes into his myth of the generations of humans, interrupting the otherwise steady degeneration represented in increasingly base (and increasingly destructive) metals. Hesiod tells us that these heroes, whose generation occurred between the violent bronze age and the depraved iron age in which Hesiod himself lives, included those who died 'fighting for the sake of Oedipus' flocks at Thebes of the seven portals' and those who went by sea to fight at Troy 'for the sake of Helen of the lovely tresses' (Sansone 58).

It is no wonder that so many myths and stories of deities include descriptions of conflict. The gods were just as hungry for power and often made mistakes in their lust for it.

Historical Context & Morality

What men or gods are these? What maidens loth?
What mad pursuit? What struggle to escape?
Ode on a Grecian Urn, by John Keats

While compiling this book, I read many translations of myths. These myths include sexual assault, violence, incest, bestiality, and other situations that could be upsetting to new (and old) readers. I admit there were times when I felt I could not read one more story of a god's sexual conquests as they sounded nonconsensual. My guess is that you might also wonder how to approach the stories with a modern mind and societal experience. (And, of course, these things happen in contemporary society too.)

Most concerning to me was the overwhelming instances of women being seen as vulnerable to the advances of male-described gods and other beings. In some stories, women were not able to escape from these situations, so they might stay with their attacker and have a child with them. Other myths describe how women who were assaulted might only escape harm by dying or by transforming into different creatures. See the story of Caenis/Kainis' attack by Poseidon.

In a 2019 master's degree thesis by Sotiria Koutsopetrou at the University of Bergen,[12] *Rape and Rape Culture in the Ancient Greek Culture? Was rape 'really' rape in Ancient Greece*? the author discusses modern rape culture and the complexities of myths that seem to abhor women being violated, while also engaging in acts of sexual assault. Koutsopetrou shows a piece of pottery depicting Theseus and Helen of Troy. In the piece, Theseus makes his desires known by facing Helen while she looks at his hand in what is described as annoyance.

Helen's image is small, which is thought to portray the frailty and weakness of women:

> On the other hand, the male actors of the mosaic dispose of the basic male characteristics of the Greek heroes. They appear energetic, self-confident, and aggressive. Their specific act is supposed to express virility, courage and determination (Koutsopetrou 34).

This image is compared with an image of the same scene as part of a mosaic. There is an apparent struggle in the mosaic, while the pottery seems to indicate coercion without violence. My modern mind and values do not see one as 'better' than the other. However, contextually, the mindset of the time could indicate that overpowering a woman was seen as an act of strength. And this art might have served to normalize these acts. It is also interesting to note that some of the myths which involve rape are myths in which a child is conceived, a child who goes on to complete heroic things. Is this another example of the desire to normalize these brutalities?

In an honor's thesis by Camryn Alwang at SUNY from 2019,[13] she speaks of cultural norms around marriage, adultery, and rape.

> In Ancient Greece, the ideal woman was one who married and bore children, especially, a male child that would continue the patriarchal family line. Families were headed by a male *kyrios*, who was the guardian of his wife, daughters, and sons, until they came of age. A woman was always under male guardianship, first under her father, then husband and upon death of her husband, her

> son. Perhaps the most important ideal in Greek society was the continuation of a family or *oikos,* demonstrated by Athenian law from the Classical Period regarding the severities of adultery and rape. Adultery, or *moicheia,* was "unauthorized sex with an Athenian woman who came under the guardianship of another Athenian citizen." In homicide legislation, the killing of the *moichos,* adulterer, was justifiable, while there is no evidence for the same in the case of a rapist (Alwang 4-5).

Not only were there different rules and standards but also men were expected to carry on their familial line no matter what. This expectation sets up the circumstances in which a man would be 'justified' in his actions to have sex with someone, even if the 'partner' did not agree to it.

In Mary Lefkowitz's 1994 paper at Wellesley College,[14] *Seduction and Rape in Greek Myth,* she challenges ideas that the myths were attempting to normalize rape culture. Her paper describes how it is not that human women were raped and abducted as much as the gods seduced them and thus did give their consent.

She notes, "Rape and seduction are regarded as equally serious crimes in the Athenian law" (Lefkowitz 20). The nuance she shares is that encounters between the humans and the gods were not typically violent. And the laws of that time stated that rape needed to include violence. Lefkowitz points out that Greeks believed that humans were not always wise about their actions, and thus, it could be understood that they made bad decisions when being with deities. The paper's ending also goes on to say that women writers of the time would likely not have been upset with the stories, as the common belief was that the gods didn't think much of humans. At the same time, the stories of the gods who showed concern for mortals and the children they bore might offer some understanding.

The translation of 'rape' might also be problematic. In Latin, *rapere*, from which 'rape' is derived, means 'robbery' or 'seizure.' In the abduction stories, there might be a miscommunication regarding how the story was told later, using rape when another word would be more accurate.

Perhaps this helps place myths into the context of the culture, but it may not. For those who want to read more, I have included additional resources at the end of this book.

I also offer the words of Sophocles, a Greek tragic playwright, in his play *Antigone*:

Many wonders, many terrors,
But none more wonderful than the human race
Or more dangerous.
This creature travels on a winter gale
Across the silver sea,
Shadowed by high-surging waves,
While on Earth, grandest of the gods,
He grinds the deathless, tireless land away,
Turning and turning the plow
From year to year, behind driven horses.

Antigone, Sophocles, translated by Paul Woodruff[15]

Chapter 2

Mythology

> One widespread usage of the word 'myth' is exemplified by a sentence such as this: 'It's a myth that all English people drink tea at four o'clock in the afternoon.' A myth, in this definition, is just 'a widely held misconception.' However, such a simplistic definition, which defines a myth in terms of its falsity, does nothing to alert us to the imaginative richness and social significance of stories and story-telling. A different and more useful kind of definition – the kind with which we shall be operating here – goes like this: 'A myth is a socially powerful traditional story' (Buxton 18).

Mythology is defined by *Merriam Webster*[16] as an allegorical narrative; a body of myths: the myths dealing with the gods, demigods, and legendary heroes of a particular people; a branch of knowledge that deals with myths; and a popular belief or assumption that has grown up around someone or something.

While Greek mythology was important in its time and the present day, these myths were not a universally agreed-upon truth. Plato, for example, criticized the myths for being untrue, while most Greek citizens believed the stories to be accurate and real.[17] Whether this is a question to consider or not, Greek mythology influenced the land, the people, the art, and the writing of the time. From the remaining writings to archaeological findings, the myths continue inspire conversation and worship.

> Greeks first experienced mythology as children, through stories told to them by their elders; mostly our sources identify the tellers as the children's nurses, mothers or grandmothers. The point of some of these tales clearly lay in social control: threatening bogey-figures such as Lamia and Gorgo were involved in getting the recalcitrant toddler to toe the line (Buxton 28).

Mythology for the Greeks spans cosmology (more in the next section), deities, time periods, seasons, heroes, and more.

Source Texts

The most frequent advice I offer to those looking to build relationships with deities or pantheons is to seek out source texts. These texts have a few subtypes: primary, secondary, and tertiary. Primary texts come directly from a person at the events described and recounted. Also known as firsthand accounts, these include stories, pictures, documents, research, and anything not previously shared or accounted for.

Secondary source texts are written based on evidence or primary texts. For example, this can be a book or story written after finding art or objects from a particular period. However, depending on the subject, objects can also be seen as primary sources. Tertiary sources are those works based on primary and secondary sources.

Some examples of sources for Greek mythology include:

- *The Library of Greek Mythology (Biblioteca),* Apollodorus
- *Epic Cycle,* various writers
    - Cypria, Stasinus
    - Aethiopis and Iliou persis, Arctinus

  - Iliad and Odyssey, Homer
  - Little Iliad, Lesches
  - Nostoi, Agias or Eumelus
  - Telegony, Eugammon

- *Homeric Hymns,* various authors (not necessarily Homer)
- *The Iliad / The Odyssey,* Homer
- *Theogony / Works and Days,* Hesiod
- *Orphic Hymns / The Hymns of Orpheus,* unclear authorship
- *Lyra Graeca (Greek Lyric I Fragments I)* – includes many poets, but the works of Alcman, Sappho, and Alcaeus are the only remaining fragments
- *Metamorphoses,* Ovid

Other authors include Aeschylus, Sophocles, Euripides, Strabo, Seneca, Virgil, and Herodotus. I describe some of the more well-known, often-cited, and popular sources in following sections.

Homer: The Iliad and The Odyssey

> The evidence indicates that the ancient Greeks experienced creative activity as an arrival from beyond the boundaries of the conscious self. In other words, poetry was not thought to be "invented" by the poet but rather "given" to the poet, sometimes whole cloth, at other times as raw material to which the poet would add a form… The poet therefore had to lose his conscious, profane self, or the fixation thereon, so that sacred imagery could pass through. The result was the religious conviction that poetry was not human but divine in origin (Hatab 60).

The epic poems of Homer, *The Iliad* and *The Odyssey,* continue to impact readers and magical practitioners. Because these texts have been translated, rewritten, and re-created in various forms, Homer has enabled ongoing connection with gods and beings as well as lessons and tragedies. For the Greeks of the time, the characters could easily overlap with their rulers, aching for power and willing to do whatever necessary to remain in leadership.

According to Nagy,[18] an epic is "an expansive poem of enormous scope, composed in an old-fashioned and superbly elevated style of language, concerning the wondrous deeds of heroes."

Nagy reminds readers that in the stories of Greek gods, there are heroes who had humans as parents, making these heroes susceptible to death. While the myths were meant to inspire wonder, some characters can die. Meanwhile, the gods are spared from the pain of death, for even when they die, it is not as 'serious' as when humans die.

There are a few things to remember regarding the Homeric poems. These poems are stories that would appeal to the common person. These poems aren't meant to be instructive in magic or ritual, and any descriptions within the texts are generally noted as incomplete or unrealistic.

> *The Iliad* takes place over a period of fifty-three days in the tenth year of the Trojan War, but only five days pass between Books 2 and 22 (out of 24 books). Although the epic is sprawling, its focus, even in time, is tight. The first word in the poem is *rage,* announcing a story about the consuming, self-destructive effects of this terrible human emotion (Morris and Powell 101).

Comparing these poems offers context for the stories they tell. While *The Iliad* speaks of the wrath of Achilles in wartime, the *The Odyssey* has been called comic, even though it is the wanderings of a man who seeks to return home and, in doing so, faces horrors and deadly encounters. "In everyday speech, we use *comic* to mean humorous, but when literary critics say comic, they mean a story that ends in harmony and acceptance" (Morris and Powell 107). While it's true that Odysseus eventually returns home and remarries Penelope, his wife, who assumed he was dead after being gone for ten years, it's not lighthearted along the way.

Some have compared *The Odyssey* to the story of Gilgamesh from Mesopotamian myth. Another man wandered across foreign lands and navigated near-death situations in a story written two thousand years before Homer's epic poem.

Hesiod: Theogony and Works and Days

Hesiod's *Theogony* and *Works and Days* (700 BCE) are source texts for myths and stories. These texts outline the family tree of the gods and related beings, which helps to create context for the interactions and better understand interpersonal relations. *Theogony* focuses more on the lineages, while *Works and Days* describes the farmer's calendar and ideas about justice. Both reveal essential thoughts of the everyday citizen while reminding the reader of deities.

Theogony is only 1000 lines and is written in the first person, as though Hesiod was on the land during the stories. Much of this poem has influenced the stories of deities in Greek mythology, but there is speculation that Hesiod may have had other motivations.

> The basileis [Mycenaean officials ranked below the king] are thus the earthy counterparts of Zeus: Just as the Muses sing the praises of Zeus and the other gods, so mortal poets like Hesiod are expected to sing the praises of the earthly basileis (along, of course, with praising

> the gods). But, unlike Zeus, the ruler of the gods, the human basileis are in need of instruction, which Hesiod is prepared to supply. Hesiod's poetry is designed to both flatter and to teach the basileis, who are expected to put up with being lectured by a poet who is their social inferior. This is because the song of the poet is felt to be a product of divine inspiration; consequently, it confers prestige on the basileus and is the most effective instrument of what today would be thought of as 'public relations' (Sansone 51).

With this thought, viewing *Theogony* as a possible condemnation of violence and power struggles in leadership is fascinating. But while the stories might serve as a disguise for social commentary, *Works and Days* is not as subtle. This poem is shorter than *Theogony*, with only 800 lines, but speaks directly to public officials by describing the difficulty of life for man.

Works and Days begins with instructions to the Muses to speak to Zeus about man.

> *Muses from Pieria, who glorify by songs, come to me, tell of Zeus your father in your singing. Because of him mortal men are unmentioned and mentioned, spoken and unspoken of, according to great Zeus' will. For easily he makes strong, and easily he oppresses the strong, easily he diminishes the conspicuous one and magnifies the inconspicuous, and easily he makes the crooked straight and withers the proud – Zeus who thunders on high, who dwells in the highest mansions. O hearken as thou seest and hearest, and make judgment straight with righteousness, Lord; while I should like to tell Perses words of truth.*

Works and Days, Hesiod, p 37, translated by M.L. West

To look at Hesiod's work from the angle of man and his apparent desire to offer a voice to the voiceless provides a different energy for the Greek mythos. Hesiod speaks to Perses, his brother, in this poem, offering him instruction in agriculture for a farm they both inherited. But, like the tragedies of the gods, Perses squandered his inheritance and returned to Hesiod after judges ruled that Perses had a right to his brother's land, too. Angry and unwilling to give his brother more, Hesiod guides him in how to work and why it is important to work.

Linear A and B

While lists of source texts for Greek mythology will often speak of Linear B, Linear A is also essential for research. Linear A is a writing system used by the Minoans before the Mycenaeans took over.[19] "It would appear that certain elements of a pre-Greek language have made their way into Greek, usually names ending in *-nthos, -ssos,* or *-eus* such as Knossos, Corinth(os), basileus, and Odysseus" (Budin 404). But this language is inaccessible as no one has been able to translate it to read it.

> The earliest written evidence for Greek language and culture, and for Greek mythology and religion, is found in economic texts on clay tablets written in a writing system known as Linear B.[20]

In Appendix One of *Anthology of Classical Myth: Primary Sources in Translation,* Palaima describes how it took fifty years for Linear B to be translated after the tablets were found in 1900 by Sir Arthur Evans at Knossos. Interestingly, these tablets were preserved because they were accidentally baked by a fire that engulfed the walls of the room they were stored in.

The Linear B writing system includes 87 phonetic signs that stand for syllables with open vowels, like pa or do. There are also about 100 ideographic signs that stand for objects or commodities. According to Palaima's *Linear B Sources* piece, there are 5000 Linear B tablets, and "The Linear B texts were written as internal administrative records that would have been consulted by officials and agents within the intensively exploitative economic systems of the period."

While there is more to be said about Linear A and B, remember that while they don't talk about rituals or myths directly, they include references to gods, including Poseidon, Zeus, Ares, Dionysus, and Hermes. While other gods are conspicuously absent, the tablets show the probable presence of deity cults. In one section, for example, there is an accounting of honey offerings to Zeus and Dionysus.

Derveni Papyrus

Ancient Greek papyrus scrolls were found in 1962, outlining details about deities and an allegorical commentary on an Orphic poem.[21] The Center for Hellenic Studies at Harvard University notes this may be the oldest Greek papyrus if not the oldest ever found.[22] One of the authors of a research paper titled *The Derveni Papyrus: An Interdisciplinary Research Project*, Kyriakos Tsantsanoglou,[23] states in the introduction that:

> The Derveni papyrus... dated roughly between 340 and 320 B.C. Its name derives from the site where it was discovered, some six miles north of Thessaloniki, in whose Archaeological Museum it is now preserved. It was found among the remnants of a funeral pyre in one of the tombs in the area... After the exacting job of unrolling and separating the layers of the charred papyrus roll, and

then of joining the numerous fragments together again, 26 columns of text were recovered, all with their bottom parts missing, as they had perished on the pyre.

The book, composed near the end of the 5th century B.C., contains the eschatological teaching of a mantis; the content is divided between religious instructions on sacrifices to gods and souls, and allegorical commentary on a theogonical poem ascribed to Orpheus. The author's outlook is philosophical, displaying, in particular, a physical system close to those of Anaxagoras, the Atomists, and Diogenes of Apollonia. His allegorical method of interpretation is especially interesting, frequently reminiscent of Socrates' playful mental and etymological acrobatics as seen in Plato's Cratylus. The identification of the author is a matter of dispute among scholars. Names like Euthyphron of Prospalta, Diagoras of Melos, and Stesimbrotus of Thasos have been proposed with varying degrees of likelihood.

These scrolls offer further proof of man's ongoing search for meaning in life, including the philosophical difficulties that come from the exploration of religion, values, and text that reads as a riddle more than a directive.

Writing Fragments

Much like the remnants of Sappho's poetry, there are fragments of writing that might serve to answer questions not already answered by Homer and Hesiod's writings.

Some of the writers include:

- Pindar of Thebes
- Aeschylus

- Sophocles
- Euripides
- Callimachus

Not only do these writings help fill gaps in other stories, but they also bring in new details to existing stories, helping to further expand and enrich the understanding of Greek myths. Later, as the Roman Empire took over, other writers like Strabo, Plutarch, and Pausanias, as mentioned previously, would offer their insights into myths, both lyrical and historical.

The Many Ways of Storytelling

> The stories that we know as 'Greek myths' were told over a wide and historically fluctuating area, by no means coincident with the territory labeled as 'Greece' on modern maps. Already by the Archaic period (conventionally 700-500 BCE), in addition to occupying the mainland north as far as Macedonia and east through Thrace to the Hellespont, Greek speakers had settled in the Aegean islands and the western seaboard of Asia Minor (in present-day Turkey). In addition, the founding of overseas settlements further afield expanded the reach of all aspects of Hellenic culture, including its stories (Buxton 19).

Within mythology, there are different categories of storytelling, depending on the type of writing and purpose.[24]

Religious Myths – The myths that focus on the gods, magic, and rituals are meant to act as religious reference points. In doing so, the gods continue to be larger than large and meant for worship and adoration.

Epics / Sagas – Another storytelling practice included more historical details and descriptions of long journeys with adventures. The stories of these epic poems and sagas outline events like the Trojan War. These stories were designed to show how heroes of the stories were real and that events of those times were accurate. In some cases, the stories were meant to show what might happen if someone didn't follow the rules of the leaders, helping justify societal rules and punishments.

Folktales – Stories were told for entertainment too, with some moral or lesson as part of the tale. There are stories of the smallest person overcoming greater powers. Or there are stories of royalty being rescued from monsters. Some of these stories were known to be fantastical, while others were retellings and re-imaginings of real life.

Poetry – While Homer's *The Iliad* and *The Odyssey* and Hesiod's *Theogony* and *Works and Days* get a lot of attention in conversations about Greek mythology; there are others, e.g., Sappho. In Classical Greece, poems were read and performed with song and dance.[25] References to Greek choruses included employing the common man instead of professional performers to act out the stories.

Art – It could be argued that Greek myth influenced art, while art might affect how stories are told and interpreted. As mentioned in a previous chapter, art revealed how gods and humans were viewed in society. Those who stood near each other were thought to be in a relationship, while those not facing each other might be in conflict. Typical art that showcased stories and myths included mosaic floors and walls, painted vases (amphora), architecture, paintings, and sculpture.

The written word is not the only possibility for stepping into mythology and its stories. With each interpretation, there are opportunities to become more immersed in the emotional landscape and its impact on culture. Artists are often conjurers of meaning and can inspire more embodied interactions with stories – interactions that can move beyond what is said and into what was felt.

Choosing Translations to Read

When expanding exploration into the Greek gods and practices, it is wise to seek out multiple versions of the myths. Because it is more common to find translations by male academics, I encourage readers to seek other translations, whenever possible.

Here are resources[26] for Hesiod and Homer's texts and Homeric Hymns:

Johnson, Kimberley. *Theogony and Works and Days*. Northwestern. 2017.
Stallings, A.E. *Works and Days*. Penguin Classics. 2018.
Alexander, Caroline. *The Iliad*. Vintage Classics. 2018.
Dacier, Anne. *Iliad*. 1699.
Dacier, Anne. *Odyssey*. 1708.
Dué, Casey and Mary Ebbott. *Iliad 10 and the Poetics of Ambush: A Multitext Edition with Essays and Commentary*. Harvard University Press. 2010.
Graziosi, Barbara and Johannes Haubold. *Iliad. Book VI. Cambridge Greek and Latin Classics*. Cambridge University Press. 2010.
Jong, Irene De. *Iliad. Book XXII*. Cambridge Greek and Latin Classics. Cambridge University Press. 2012.
Rayor, Diane J. *The Homeric Hymns*. University of California Press. 2014.

Ruden, Sarah. *Homeric Hymns*. Hackett. 2005.
Wilson, Emily. *The Iliad*. W.W. Norton & Company. 2023.
Wilson, Emily. *The Odyssey*. W.W. Norton & Company. 2017.

Another way to approach engagement with Greek myths is to consider reading different versions of each story. From one translation to another, you can find differences that might reveal the translator's bias or choices of words as a reflection of the era in which they were translated. In either situation, exposing yourself to what is available and remaining curious about how it might inform your magical practices is valuable.

For those wanting to explore the ancient Greek language (which is different from modern Greek), it is worthwhile to find original Greek texts and see how they are translated into modern English or other languages. Reviewing the potential word choices and how deities are described can help you better understand how they appear in myths. Even if you cannot decipher complete texts on your own, you might use available translation technology to get a view of what arrived on the pages.

Chapter 3

Cosmology & Cosmogony

Above the cloud with its shadow is the star with its light. Above all things reverence thyself. Pythagoras

Because these two words are so close in form, let's compare them to see how they relate and differ to better understand their placement in a conversation about the Greek pantheon. The word ***kosmos*** is Greek for "order, ornament, world or universe."[27] According to *Oxford Reference,* cosmology is "The world view and belief system of a community based upon their understanding of order in the universe."[28] This idea initially came from Pythagoras, a mathematician who wanted to describe the universe's structure.[29]

There is also 'cosmogony,' which is "the theory of the origin of the universe; the creation or origin of the world or universe,"[30] So cosmology and cosmogony are related in ways that may seem subtle but are also important. To make it simpler, remembering there is always nuance in complicated ideas, here is what I offer to better hold these two concepts:

Cosmology – how the universe began, which informs views and beliefs, often beyond science.
Cosmogony – how the universe began, from more of a scientific viewpoint.

A Story of Creation

What you will notice in Greek mythology is that the story of the creation of the universe does not take up a lot of space in the epic poems.

First came the Chasm; and then broad-breasted Earth, secure seat for ever of all the immortals who occupy the peak of snowy Olympus; the misty Tartara in a remote recess of the broad-pathed earth; and Eros, the most handsome among the immortal gods, dissolver of flesh, who overcomes the reason and purpose in the breasts of all gods and all men.

Out of the Chasm came Erebos and dark Night, and from Night in turn came Bright Air and Day, whom she bore in shared intimacy with Erebos. Earth bore first of all one equal to herself, starry Heaven, so that he should cover her all about, to be a secure seat for ever for the blessed gods; and she born the long Mountains, pleasant haunts of the goddesses, the Nymphs who dwell in mountain glens; and she bore also the undraining Sea and its furious swell, not in union of love But then, bedded with Heaven, she bore deep-swirling Oceanus.

Theogony, Hesiod, pp 6-7, translated by M.L. West

This story is often retold as creation being born out of chaos, but the translation here is 'chasm,' which certainly could have been a chaotic process. Still, it is not associated with the disorder but is often associated with chaotic moments. Instead, Chaos and Chasm are the void from which life arrived – and is similar to other culture's creation stories.

Note that Earth is the name for Gaia, who birthed the building blocks of the universe to give way to the gods. From the Chasm/ Chaos is born, according to *Theogony*, the primordial gods include:

Gaia – Earth
Tartarus – Abyss
Eros – Desire
Erebus – Dark
Nyx – Night

I offer this simple list to get a sense of how they are connected in a complicated and widely debated family tree (as Hesiod wrote). This is the start of the genealogy of the gods, and the other connections between gods by parentage, children, consort, or violence are seen in Part II.

→ = gave birth to
+ = married to / consort of

Gaia → Uranus (Sky)
Gaia → Pontus (Sea) and Ourea (Mountains)
Gaia + Pontus → Thaumas (Wonder), Eurybia (Master of the Sea), Nereus (Old Man of the Sea)
Gaia + Uranus → Cyclopes, Hecantoncheires, Titans (Oceanus, Tethys, Hyperion, Theia, Crius,
Coeus, Phoebe, Iapetus, Cronus, Rhea, Themis, Mnemosyne)
→ Aphrodite (from Uranus' severed genitals)
→ Furies, Giants & Nymphs (from blood from severed genitals that fell on Gaia)
Tartarus + Gaia → Typhon (Hurricane) → Typhus (Wind)
Eros (primordial god) – no children, not to be confused with Aphrodite's son, born by Ares
Erebus + Nyx → Aether (Light) and Hemera (Day)
→ Moros (Doom), Ker (Death Fate), Thanatos/Thanatus (Death), Hypnos/Hypnus (Sleep), Oneiriri
(Dreams), Momus (Blame), Oizys (Misery), The Hesperides, Moirae (Fates),
Keres (Deaths), Nemesis (Indignation), Apate (Deceit), Philotes (Sex), Geras
(Old Age), Eris (Strife)

Theogony informs the family tree of the Greek gods as it is the oldest and most complete piece of writing to survive, but other accounts offer different stories.

> According to Homer's *Iliad* she [Aphrodite] was born, not from the severed genitals of Ouranos, but by a more orthodox route: her parents were Zeus and the goddess Dione, a little-known figure for whom our most extensive evidence relates to her role as Zeus' consort at the oracle of Dodona in Epeiros. Homer's genealogy thus shifts the emphasis away from Aphrodite-as-cosmic-principle to Aphrodite-as-anthropomorphic-deity. Indeed the Homeric Aphrodite is all too human: when wounded in the hand by the mortal hero Diomedes, *this* Aphrodite rushes from the battlefield to be comforted by her mother, like a child who has hurt herself in the playground (Buxton 49).

The Derveni Papyrus:

> ...ascribes a fundamental role in creation to a divine figure who preceded not only Ouranos but even Night. This figure is referred to sometimes as Protogonos ('First Born'), sometimes as Phanes ('The One who Makes to Appear' or 'The One who Appears'), and sometimes under other names (Eros, Bromios, Erikepaios, Metis, Zeus) as befits one who incorporates all existence within himself (Buxton 52).

Buxton describes how the very firstborn emerged from a cosmic egg created by Time as a fully formed bisexual being. Protogonos held all possibilities and probabilities for children and beings in this form.

Realms of the Gods

The gods arrive with stories, lovers, and adventures across different realms. While Olympus is one of the realms of gods, it is not the only one, even though it is the most frequently mentioned and thus more easily remembered.

The Greek myths describe the stories of the gods and other beings across different realms: Sky, Sea, and Underworld. After the 10-year Titanomachy conflict,[32] Zeus, Poseidon, and Hades drew lots to see who would get each realm. As a result of the lots, Zeus was given the Sky, Poseidon was given the sea, and Hades was given the underworld to rule.

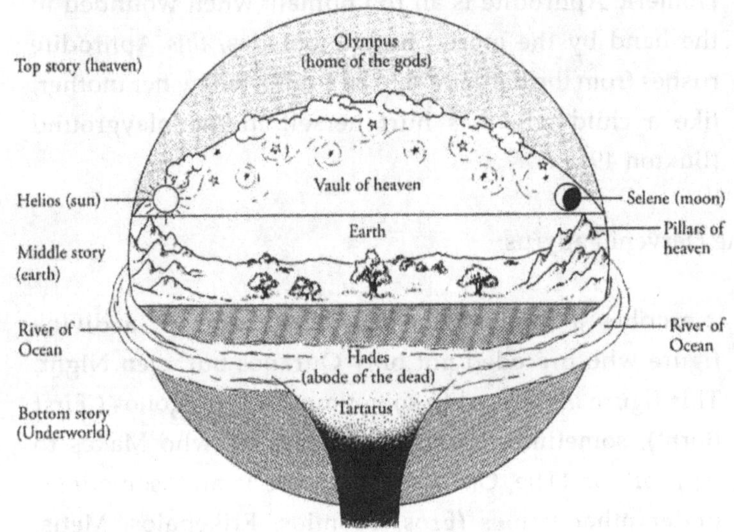

Map of Ancient Greek Realms[32]

Each of these places had its responsibilities and challenges, but it was assumed that Zeus was the ruler over all these realms, which plays out in the stories and adventures.

Sky

Now the gods were seated in assembly by Zeus' side
on a floor of fold; and among them lady Hebe
poured nectar, and with goblets of gold

they pledged one another, looking down upon the city of the Trojans.

The Iliad, Homer, Book 4, 1-4, translated by Caroline Alexander

The Sky is a heavenly place is held up by four pillars, which include four of the Titans (Coeus, Crius, Hyperion, and Iapetus). In this realm was Mount Olympus, one of the most easily recognized places in mythology, a place above the clouds and the stars. This palatial structure sat on a hill from which the deities could watch over the mortals. Golden gates were guarded by the Horai[33] and Zeus lived in a grand palace. Less important deities also had dwellings. Along with the gods lived the Muses and horses, including the winged Pegasus.

Divine beings gathered in courtyard in front of Zeus' acropolis. *The Iliad* describes structures as made of stone and bronze, with the same features as traditional Greek homes, e.g., hallways, bedrooms, etc. There were golden floors where the gods feasted and made decisions. No one was allowed through the doors to Olympus unless the gods gave them permission.

Sea

On open roads they crossed the Ocean stream,
went past the rock of Leucas and the gates
of Helius the Sun, and skittered through
the provinces of dreams, and soon arrived
in fields of asphodel, the home of shadows
who have been worn to the weariness of life.

The Odyssey, Homer, Book 24, 11-16, translated by Emily Wilson

Poseidon ruled the sea as a realm of water and islands that encircled the cosmos. This realm contained the places for the dead to travel as a reward for mighty feats.

Elysium / Elysian Fields – Heroes would go to the Elysian Fields after being killed in battle. Sometimes known as the Islands of the Blessed, these were in the western stream of the river of Oceanus and ruled by Cronus.
Erytheia – Also known as the Red Isle, Erytheia was an island in the western stream of Oceanus. The red coloring came from the light of the sunset. It was home to the three-bodied Geryon, a giant with red-hided cattle.
Oceanus – While Oceanus is also described as a deity, this was the freshwater river that surrounded the Earth and gave water to all rivers, springs, etc. Often described as related to the flow of time, Oceanus stretched to the edge of the cosmos and held the curve of the sky above in place.

Underworld

[Traveling to Hades]
We reached the sea and first of all we launched
the ship into the sparkling salty water,
set up the mast and sails, and brought the sheep
on board with us. We were still grieving, weeping,
in floods of tears. But beautiful, dread Circe,
the goddess who can speak in human tongues,
sent us a wind to fill our sails, fair wind
befriending us behind the dark blue prow.
We made our tackle shipshape, then sat down.
The wind and pilot guided straight our course.
The sun set. It was dark in all directions.

The Odyssey, Homer, Book 11, 1-11, translated by Emily Wilson

Hades was the ruler and leader of the underworld and the embodiment of the underworld, which was the final resting place for the dead. Located at the ends of the Earth, the underworld was at the far shore of Oceanus. While important in the landscape of deities, he was not considered an Olympian, nor was his bride, Persephone, as they were located far away from Olympus.

Acherusian/Akherousian Lake surrounded the land of the dead and was the route souls took to the underworld ferried by Charon/Kharon.[34] Hermes brought the souls from Earth to this place as a psychopomp, delivering them to Minos, the judge, to be sentenced to an afterlife of torment. Extending from this lake were five rivers: Acheron, Kokytos/Cocytus, Pyriphlegethon, Lethe, and Styx.

Acheron – The River of Pain was the entrance to the lower world, also known as the river of Hades.

Kokytos/Cocytus – The River of Wailing.

Pyriphlegethon – The River of Fire.

Lethe – The River of Oblivion.

River Styx – The most well-known river was Styx. The gods used its corrosive water to make sacred promises. Iris would travel to the river and gather the water in a pitcher to distribute to the gods during oath making. Anyone who made a promise with this water and did not keep it would be banished from feasts and gatherings for nine years. The icy water trickled down from a high rocky place. In the *Aeneid*, the river Styx wrapped around the borders of Hades nine times.

Tartarus

[Zeus warns the gods to not defy him in war]
And anyone I perceive against the gods' will attempting
to go among the Trojans and help them, or among the Danaäns,
he shall go whipped against his dignity back to Olympos;
or I shall take him and dash him down to the murk of Tartaros,
far below, where the uttermost depth of the pit lies under
earth, where there are gates of iron and a brazen doorstone,
as far beneath the house of Hades as from earth the sky lies.

The Iliad, Homer, Book 8, 10-16, translated by Richmond Lattimore

While positioned at the bottom of the world, Tartarus is not the underworld. Instead, this is a pit of punishment, and where the Titans were sent after their defeat. Because Tartarus is often described in hell-like terms, this has led to confusion, often unfairly aligning it with an underworld setting. This place of isolation is surrounded by a wall of bronze with gates guarded by the Hekatonkheires.[35]

Additional Ancient Greek Perspectives on the Universe

Understanding the way Greeks saw the world(s) can inform the way stories have been told and interpreted later, and it can help us learn a little about how science saw the universe.

Thales of Miletus, an ancient philosopher, thought things seen as mystical had a scientific explanation. Thales believed water was the primary building block of the universe; thus, everything was built from it.[36] This all-important water, he proposed, surrounded a flat disk of Earth, which floated within it. At the same time, he was likely the first to predict eclipses and to conceptualize the idea of a sphere around the top of the earth with stars and planets.

In Miletus, Anaximander, who studied with Thales, proposed that the universe was made from a primal substance called Apeiron (boundlessness).[37] He thought the Earth was shaped like a cylinder and floated in space. Miletus believed the Earth, Moon, and stars all rotated around each other, moved by air, with the Earth as the center.

Aristarchus of Samos brought these ideas of science further with the idea of a heliocentric model of the universe, or a universe with the sun at the center. He also figured out how to measure the sizes of and distances between the planets.[38]

The difference between these ideas and the worlds shown in the lyrical poetry of Hesiod and Homer demonstrates the desire to explain the world. Creating order through myths and theories seems a common feature of civilizations striving to understand their place in history. And while there are mistakes along the way, creating sense is not about coming to a final answer.

While many more influenced how the Greeks saw the universe, including Ptolemy, Pythagoras, and more, it is interesting that poems and stories of the deities reference the idea of a round Earth.

GREAT Heav'n, whose mighty frame no respite knows,
Father of all, from whom the world arose:
Hear, bounteous parent, source and end of all,
Forever whirling round this ***earthly ball****;*

III: To Heaven, The Orphic Hymns, translated by Thomas Taylor

Or in this hymn to Earth or Gaia:

From whose wide womb, as from an endless root,
Fruits, many-form'd, mature and grateful shoot.
Deep bosom'd, blessed, pleas'd with grassy plains,

Sweet to the smell, and with prolific rains.
All flow'ry dæmon, centre of the world,
***Around thy orb**, the beauteous stars are hurl'd*
With rapid whirl, eternal and divine,
Whose frames with matchless skill and wisdom shine.

XXV: To the Earth, The Orphic Hymns, translated by Thomas Taylor

While the astronomers and philosophers of the time may not have agreed upon the structure of the Earth or its placement, it was clear the poets may have understood something beyond logic.

Chapter 4

Religion & Ritual

> [T]here was another side to Greek religion. They knew that gods abounded everywhere: these powers could be friendly, but they could equally well be indifferent or positively hostile. You had to be careful: to avoid arousing a god's opposition was as important as winning his support. This helps to explain why religion played such a large part in Greek life. Prayers, sacrifices, omens, oracles, festivals, buildings, all were reminders of the gods. This religion was more concerned with ritual than morals. What was important was to make the right sacrifices to the right god at the right place with the right words. If you did, you could, as Plato complained, be wicked and get away with it. Of course good behaviour was desirable; but it was more for the sake of your family, friends and fellow-citizens than for the gods (Amos and Lang 71).

In ancient Greece, there were no designations for specific religions. As described, there were practices a person did to appease the gods and to ensure successful harvests, battles, marriages, and more. People followed practices based on what they were taught, where they lived, and what was most important to them. In doing so, the people could remain in the favor of the gods, and be rewarded.

Stanley Spaeth Barbette states:

> There was no centralization of authority over Greek religious practices and beliefs; change was regulated only

> at the civic level. Thus, the phenomenon we are studying is not, in fact, an organized 'religion.' Instead we might think of the beliefs and practices of Greeks in relation to the gods as a group of closely related 'religious dialects' that resembled each other far more than they did those of non-Greeks.[39]

With that in mind, one can better see and understand the beliefs of ancient Greece and the practices and rituals used most often. How people acted speaks to their understanding of the universe, their part to play and the power they did (or did not) have.

Offerings

Offerings were common practices in ancient Greece and many ancient cultures. Giving something valuable to a god was to honor them and show your devotion. Libations and animal sacrifices are mentioned in the epic poems of the time and are seen in imagery on pottery.

Offerings included wheat, bread, barley, fruit, flowers, cake, and other delights as the gods instructed and desired. After all, whatever a god requested from humans would be given and offered at their temple and celebrations.

Libations

> *...Eurylochus*
> *and Perimedes made the sacrifice.*
> *I drew my sword and dug a hole, a cubit*
> *widthways and lengthways, and I poured libations*
> *for all the dead: first honey-mix, sweet wine,*
> *and lastly, water. On the top, I sprinkled*
> *barley, and made a solemn vow that if*
> *I reached my homeland, I would sacrifice*

my best young heifer, still uncalved, and pile
the altar high with offerings for the dead.
I promised for Tiresias as well
a pure black sheep, the best in all my flock.
So with these vows, I called upon the dead.
I took the sheep and slit their throats above
the pit. Black blood flowed out. The spirits came
up out of Erebus and gathered round.

The Odyssey, Homer, Book 11, 22-37, translated by Emily Wilson

Odysseus poured honey, milk, wine, water, and white barley meal into a hole in the earth, at Circe's instruction, as a libation. Pouring into the earth so that the dead might know the offering, this libation, along with the animal sacrifice, was a typical practice.

Honey, milk, wine, and water were typical libations, but olive oil or blood from battle were also used. These offerings were given at the start or completion of meals, often with prayers or words for the gods. These libations could be provided for a specific purpose or aim, including reinforcing prayer.

> *[Dionysus says:] Three bowls do I mix for the temperate: one to health, which they empty first; the second to love and pleasure; the third to sleep. When this bowl is drunk up, wise guests go home. The fourth bowl is ours no longer, but belongs to violence; the fifth to uproar; the sixth to drunken revel; the seventh to black eyes; the eighth is the policeman's; the ninth belongs to biliousness; and the tenth to madness and the hurling of furniture.*[40]

According to Connelly,[41] libations could be directly poured onto the earth or an altar from shallow bowls or wine jugs. These libations were used alongside animal sacrifice or in place of that practice. If you used both, the combination of devotion would be a powerful addition to a ritual.

Sacrifice – Animal and Pharmakos

Animal sacrifices were a commonplace and solemn offering in ancient Greece. Sometimes combined with libations, sacrifices included cows, pigs, sheep, and other domesticated animals from someone's fields.

It would be a great sacrifice (from the word *sacer*, or to make holy) to offer an animal that could be food or produce food for the gods. Sometimes, the animals were raised solely for sacrifice. All animal parts might be offered to the gods, or the inedible parts might remain on an altar, while the participants ate the remaining meat in celebration. While the animal parts might be left as offerings in their wholeness, other rituals and offerings might require them to be burned completely.

Pharmakos, or human sacrifice, was performed during difficult times in a community where the gods needed a more important offering. In *The Ancient Greeks Sacrificed Ugly People* by Dania Rodriguez, the author notes:

> In early Greek history, during times of plague or famine, when the precarious agrarian societies started to fear for their survival, each Greek town would elect its ugliest inhabitant, known as the pharmakos. ('Ugly' in this case probably meant deformed in some way, and certainly from the fringes of society. An aristocrat with a big nose would not qualify.) For a while, this person would be fed at public expense with the most exquisite delicacies available at the time – figs, barley cakes and cheese. Afterwards, he or she (or they – some places, like

Athens, would choose... a man and a woman) would be driven through the town while being violently smote with leeks and wild plants by a wrathful mob. This ugly unfortunate's fate largely depended on the town's own tradition. In some places he or she was merely cast out of the city, while in others the pharmakos would be stoned to death, burned, or thrown off a cliff.

How popular was this ritual? In some places, so popular that it became annual. In Athens, for instance, it was celebrated during the yearly Thargelia festival.[42]

While this ritual became less focused on death and more on punishment over time, the connection between offering and respect paid to a god was clear. The more you sacrificed, the more serious your petition might be supported in your life. And while these offerings did not guarantee your success, they afforded you the best chance of blessings.

Oathmaking

In the Homeric language *hórkos* designates every kind of oath: the type which gives a guarantee of what one is going to do, a pact; or else the type which supports a statement relating to the past, the so-called judiciary oath. Thus the sense of *hórkos* does not depend on the nature of the oath.

But it is important to note that the Homeric *hórkos* is not an act of speech. Let us read the formula of the "great oath" of the gods: 'May Earth and the vast Sky above and the waters of the Styx which go down (to the lower world), which is the strongest oath for the blessed gods, be witnesses' (*Il.*15, 36ff).

Cf. [In comparison] The Homeric Hymn to Demeter 259: "May the *hórkos* of the gods, the implacable waters of the Styx, be witness." Here the "*hórkos* of the gods" is put in apposition with *húdōr* 'water': it is the water of the Styx which is the *hórkos*.

> Hesiod, in fact, in the *Theogony* (l. 400) makes the Styx into a nymph whom Zeus wished to honor by making her "the great *hórkos* of the gods." This is why Zeus, when he wants to find out which of the gods has lied (l. 784f.), sends Iris far away to bring back the "great *hórkos* of the gods" in an ewer. This is the famous water which flows cold from a steep and precipitous rock, the water of Styx. We see, then, that the water of Styx by itself constitutes the *hórkos* of the gods, being a material invested with baneful powers.[43]

Oaths are a sacred act of the gods, in which water from the water of Styx is drunk to seal oaths. Those who do not maintain their oaths are punished and driven out of Olympus for a period. Oathmaking showed up in rituals and even the Olympic Games in ancient Greece.

Like prayers and other practices, oathmaking required not only the declaration of what the oath included but also a reference to the deity or recipient to bless and make sacred.

Death & Funeral Rites

Before the invention of modern funerary practices, death was a family matter handled in the home. The body was washed and anointed with oil to prepare for the underworld journey. The deceased was laid out for others to view, with coins on their eyes as payment to Charon/Kharon, the ferryman, for bringing them safely into the afterlife.

Female relatives of the deceased wailed loudly as the body was presented, thrashing about and ripping their hair and clothing in their grief. The person was buried or cremated after visitors offered them libations, prayers, and a lock of hair. Often, there would be a feast with the closest relatives and another washing of the body. After death, the dead continued to be celebrated, with libations poured into the ground, and the dead were remembered again at larger festivals.

However, Solon, a politician in Athens, changed the rules to remove women from these roles.

> Solon's laws were also intended to control public appearances of women, including their expression of private emotion in public... Solon's legislation of funerals prescribed that only close kin could mourn for the dead, thus prohibiting the ostentatious practice among the aristocracy of hiring women mourners and denying older women a source of income (Fantham, Elaine, et al. 76).

Grave sites were also utilized to call attention to the honor of war and war heroes.

> The war graves had altar-like dressed stone monuments topped with statues and ten inscribed stone casualty lists, and, at least in 394 B.C., a sculpted frieze. In Homer's eighth-century epics, the monumental tomb helped to create the deathless glory of the individual hero; in fifth-century Athens this was turned on its head, with households refraining from elaborate markers, while the *polis* used the tomb to create a communal ideal (Morris 131).

Morris also discusses the challenges of moving between archaeological sites and what they show about death and ritual, illuminating how the social structures influenced death rites.

This thought offers a moment of introspection, as what remains of the past can sometimes seem to be the whole truth, but there are inferences in the remains that warrant speculation. While the stories of the gods might say something about belief, they might also offer something about society as much as they might offer about religion.

Weddings & Marriage

To create context for marriage[44] in parts of ancient Greece, men would typically not be married until they were around 30, while girls would be married at 15 years of age. This allowed for the transition of men into the political landscape while the girls married as a rite of passage into adulthood.[45]

The marriage ritual began days before the rite and differed based on the location. In Athens, weddings were multi-day events, with the bride preparing for her wedding by spending time with her female relatives, an event called Proaulia. During this time, the bride would make offerings to Aphrodite, Athena, and Artemis.

> [O]n fifth-century Athenian vases the bride is depicted as being adorned by other women with the help of Eros and other companions of Aphrodite and sometimes by Aphrodite herself (Price 96-97).

Gamos, the wedding day, ritualized the transfer of the bride from her father's care to her groom. The bride started with a purification bath, and the couple made offerings together to ensure a lasting relationship. Then, they would go to a feast at the groom's family house. Once the feast was over, the bride was taken by chariot to the groom's home, where she would be taken in, given gifts, and have her veil removed by her groom in his bedroom to complete the ritual. Epaulia was the final step in these marriages, with people visiting with gifts to celebrate the relationship, the sexual partnership, and the home.

In Sparta,[46] things were different, with fewer rituals than in Athens, but there was a more intricate ritual with the bride being visited by her groom at night, repeatedly. The bride would consent to being captured, even having her head shaved, and be laid in a dark room. Her groom would sneak in to see her and lay with her but had to return to the barracks before dawn. Some sources describe this back-and-forth happening so many times that the couple would have children before meeting in the daylight.

Mystery Cults

The mystery cults of Ancient Greece were aptly named as their practices remained secret and hidden. The goings-on in these cults were only known by initiates who had dedicated their lives to learning the mysteries and acting in service to the temple and the gods. Unlike day-to-day practices, these cults offered opportunities to have deeply mystical experiences where one could interface with the gods. These cults also offered ways to learn about religion and the afterlife.

> Cults of female divinities regularly had priestesses as their chief personnel, but, like their male counterparts, these women were not chosen for extraordinary piety or after special religious training. Generally the priesthood was either hereditary within a family or was 'bought' by a wealthy family for one of its members, for a limited term in office (Fantham et al. 93).

Two of the most notable mystery cults were that of Eleusis and Dionysus. While Eleusis was location-based, the Dionysian cults were more widespread.

Eleusinian Mysteries

> *Thrice happy are those of mortals, who having seen those rites depart for Hades; for to them alone is it granted to have true life there; to rest all there is evil.* Sophocles[47]

This mystery cult followed the journey of Demeter and Persephone to the underworld each fall (Greater Mysteries) and followed the return from Hades each spring (Lesser Mysteries). Based on the story of the abduction of Persephone by Hades, this cult followed the descent to the underworld, the search for Persephone, and the ascent that reunited Demeter with Persephone, as promised. Considered an agrarian mystery that followed the growth and death of the seasons, the Eleusinian Mysteries were likely inspired by previous Minoan rites and religious practices.

These mysteries reenacted the journey of Demeter, who stopped at a well during her search for Persephone, and cult initiates into the mysteries would do the same. These practitioners would drink barley and mint, which may have offered hallucinogenic effects, creating perfect conditions for spiritual ecstasy and communion with gods. Once the drink began to take effect, the initiates would go to the Telesterion, an underground theater, and watch the story of Persephone and Demeter before returning to the surface. In witnessing the death and rebirth of Kore (her name when Persephone was young) and Persephone (when she was of adult age), the initiates could understand the afterlife better and would forget any fears of death.

Dionysian Mysteries

> *Blessed, blessed are those who know the mysteries of god.*
> *Blessed is he who hallows his life in the worship of god,*

he whom the spirit of god possesseth, who is one
with those who belong to the holy body of god.
Blessed are the dancers and those who are purified,
who dance on the hill in the holy dance of god.
Blessed are they who keep the rite of Cybele the Mother.
Blessed are the thyrsus-bearers, those who wield in their hands
the holy wand of god.
Blessed are those who wear the crown of the ivy of god.
Blessed, blessed are they: Dionysus is their god!

The Bacchae, Euripides, translated by Gilbert Murray[48]

Like the Eleusinian Mysteries, the Dionysian Mysteries also related to death and rebirth. As Dionysius is connected to wine, wild abandon, and ecstasy, these mysteries encouraged participants to lose themselves in wine and dance. Initiates in these mysteries would go into trance-like states to follow Dionysus into the underworld, where they learned about true liberation from civilization and its constraints to ascend into a wider knowing and understanding of themselves.

The wine was likely mixed with other psychoactive drugs, including poppy (the source of opium). However, the introduction of altered states was also enhanced by music and dance, guiding the participants into the body and out of the head. During the rites, spirits possessed priests, further connecting into the wildness where the participants might more easily access joy and delight.

Since these rituals were not confined to one area, each would be influenced by the lands and the peoples of those lands. As mystery cults, some practices have been lost to that secrecy, but one can infer activities from the hymns and writings about Dionysus and his followers. And there is strong evidence these mysteries were open to men and women, as well as to marginalized groups of slaves, non-citizens, and criminals.

Oracles

Rapidly then the lord's courage and resplendent limbs grew; and when the due time came round, the great crooked-schemer Kronos, tricked by the cunning counsel of Earth, defeated by his son's strength and stratagem, brought his brood back up.

Theogony, Hesiod, pp 17-18, translated by M. L. West

The more you read about ancient Greece, the more you find stories of oracles and prophecy. An oracle could see into the future and was called on for advice or counsel. In the story of Psyche and Eros, Psyche's parents turned to the oracle when their daughter could not find a husband.

According to some sources, Gaia, the primordial mother, was the first oracle, offering direction to those she birthed. Oracles were also thought to be able to relay messages from the gods to humans, acting as a conduit for direct communication.

Two oracles were as important to ancient Greece: Pythia and the oracle of Dione and Zeus.

Pythia[49]

Pythia, the Oracle at Delphi and priestess of Apollo, spoke the words of Apollo and was considered a high (if not the highest) authority in ancient Greece. Pythia would speak to politicians, leaders, visitors, philosophers, and more about political issues, war, family matters, law, and any issues of importance.

Pythia was tested in her powers of prophecy and deemed the most accurate by the King of Lydia, Croesus. While her prophecies were not always accurate, those who sought her out would dismiss these mistakes as errors of human interpretation. When the king of Lydia asked Pythia about a battle, he was told that a great empire would be destroyed. While the King was confident in his soldiers and deemed this message a positive one, his side lost the battle.

Apollo possessed the priestess and then answered questions. Some descriptions of the priestess include her sitting over a hole in the ground with vapors rising, but there are few reliable sources to help someone understand how the oracle worked. What seems true is that there were many oracles, with Pythia being the name taken on by the next oracle when the previous one died. This role of a priestess was respected and honored and seen to be a valuable career for a woman at that time. Within the temple of an oracle were attendants who supported the Pythia, took care of her, and helped her with her role. The original Pythia continued to hold importance over many years until her last recorded message in 362 CE.

Oracle of Dione and Zeus

The Oracle of Dione and Zeus at Dodona was in a grove of oak trees and considered the oldest of the oracles. At this site, priests were tasked with relaying messages from the gods, though priestesses stepped into the role later.

Other oracles were also present, including Sibyl at Cumae and oracles at Didyma and Abae.

Temples

> The sacred way leading to the temple of Apollo at Delphi was lined with miniature temples, conventionally called 'treasuries,' that had been erected by victorious Greek states from the spoils filched from vanquished Greek states, because Apollo was invoked as a god of victory whenever states entered the fray (Garland 200).

Temples (***ναός* / *naos***) celebrated the gods. They were the internal dwellings of larger areas called sanctuaries and were mainly used to store offerings to the gods instead of being meeting or celebration spaces. Because many sanctuaries and temples have been destroyed, there is some confusion about their history. Some sources note that sanctuaries were built first, often alongside caves or other natural structures, with temples arriving later as they were expensive to build.

Once made of wood, temples were eventually built with stone to be more resilient in the natural elements. These temples were built in every large city, or polis, and temples began to arrive in Delphi and Olympia between the 6th and 4th centuries BCE. The rectangle with columns around the sides is the most recognized shape, but there were other temple structures. Designs depended on the builders, the materials, and the time. Temples were often built over older temples, confusing those who found them later. Parts of different structures could be hard to discern and identify.

Listing all ancient temples would be impossible, as many fell into decay or were destroyed during battles. You might also see the idea of *ὁ ναός*, or ***ho naós***, versus the word 'temple,' as this refers to temples as dwellings of the divine. Here are some prominent temples dedicated to Greek deities:

- Temples of Apollo – Corinth, Delphi
- Temple of Artemis – Corfu
- Temple of Athena (Nike) – Athens
- Temple of Hephaestus – Athens
- Temple of Heras – Corfu, Olympia
- Temple of Poseidon (Isthmia) – Corinth
- Temple of Zeus – Olympia
- The Parthenon – Athens

There are many more temples extending beyond the borders of Greece into Italy, Sicily, and beyond, showing the reach of the gods and their influence.

Olympic Games

While one might watch the Olympic Games today and see references to the gods, the games in ancient Greece combined ritual and religion. The Olympic Games were an event dedicated to Zeus, and a part of a larger festival dedicated to the king of the gods held every four years.

> Surviving inscriptions and literary sources list the names of about eight hundred ancient Olympic champions; the first recorded victor was Koroibos of Elis, who won the stadion (footrace) in 776 B.C. By the sixth century B.C., Panhellenic games – from pan (all) and hellenikos (Greek) – were also held at Delphi, Nemea, and Isthmia and attracted athletes from all over the Greek world... Each Panhellenic festival was marked by a truce, or ekecheiria, which literally means "holding of hands." Inscribed on a bronze diskos displayed at Olympia, the truce not only allowed athletes and fans to travel safely, but also provided a common basis for peace among the Greeks.[50]

Greek deities were the first competitors in the games, with Apollo racing and beating Hermes. Ares lost to Apollo during a fight. Zeus wrestled his father, Cronus, for power.

As the games were in dedication and celebration of the gods, it was custom to have animal sacrifices of 100 oxen[51] and prayers and offerings to the gods from athletes to support their success. Like other rites, the Olympics included a procession into the games, and athletes made oaths and testified to their rigorous training and preparation.

Personal Practice

> If we recall the existential meaning of the sacred in a mythical world, we can well understand such a form

> of intimacy – but the preoccupation with beauty and joy, visual and sensual delight, is perhaps nowhere so pronounced as in Greek religion (Hatab 55).

The daily personal practices of citizens were individual and ongoing. Anyone was able to visit temples and leave offerings or say prayers. Those who needed healing might travel to the temple of Asclepius or Apollo. Homes had hearths sacred to Hestia and the flame of the gods. People arranged sacrifices of animals at temples.

Because stories of the gods were a part of daily life, even from birth, the everyday person associated actions or inactions to the will of the gods. It was customary to interpret things as being the will of the gods, possibly as omens or blessings. There were gods for every aspect of daily life, and their energies were woven into decision-making. Unlike modern society, there wasn't a separation of church and state as the gods were in the places of worship and the places of governance.

According to *Daily Life of the Ancient Greeks*, each household would have their own religion, and the head of the household would act as the high priest, typically the eldest son.

> It was his duty to perform all the rituals pertaining to the welfare and prosperity of the household, in particular by making offerings, perhaps on a daily basis, to the three deities who were believed to safeguard its security and prosperity (Garland 134).

Notably, as outlined in the next section, festivals and celebrations are key examples of the gods being a priority and driving force in everyday life.

Chapter 5

Celebrations & Festivals

> In Greek, *thea* can mean a goddess and also something seen, and the later developments of tragic drama find their religious roots in this earlier sense of a *theatron*, a spectacle for divine onlookers. Therefore the festive scenes of divine and human gatherings have a serious religious significance. We should not think of the feasts and sacrifices of the Greek cults as primarily utilitarian requests or appeasement but rather a form of convocation. Religious references are always filled with invitations, summonings, and songs of advent, so that the gods can become present (unconcealed), *seen*, and therefore known (Hatab 55).

Festivals for the gods provided ongoing evidence of connection between the gods and everyday life. Preparations for and celebrations of deities maintained the focus on the gods and their importance, but these celebrations varied across cities and groups. Exact dates are tricker to find due to following a lunar calendar versus the modern solar calendar.

While there are a few calendar types for this time, this is a standard listing of the months of the ancient Greek calendar,[52] and each month would start on a new moon:

1. Hekatombaion / **Ἑκατομβαιών** – July – August
2. Metageitnion / **Μεταγειτνιών** – August – September
3. Boidromion / **Βοηδρομιών** – September – October
4. Pyanopsion / **Πυανεψιών** – October – November

5. Maimakterion / **Μαιμακτηριών** – November – December
6. Poseidon / **Ποσιδεών** – December – January
7. Gamelion / **Γαμηλιών** – January – February
8. Anthesterion / **Ἀνθεστηριών** – February – March
9. Elaphebolion / **Ἐλαφηβολιών** – March – April
10. Mounikhion / **Μουνυχιών** – April – May
11. Thargelion / **Θαργηλιών** – May – June
12. Skirophorion / **Σκιροφοριών** – June – July

As you will notice, some of the months were also the names of (or similar to the names of) the festivals below due to their timing and annual occurrences.

Panathenaea – Seen as the beginning of the year, in the month of Hekatombaion (meaning hecatomb or 100), Panathenaea included a procession of bulls to be sacrificed. This celebration was dedicated to Athena, who guarded the city of Athens. Panathenaea was another word for 'all-Athenian' as it was a festival anyone and everyone could participate in.

Metageitnia – In honor of Apollo, Metageitnia included sacrifices and feasts while celebrating the emigration of people from Melite to Diomis.

Boedromia – This celebration of Apollo focused on the political and military aspects of the god while honoring the role of the gods in helping to guide battles to victory or favorable outcomes.

Pyanepsia – This festival for Apollo focused on the story of Theseus' challenge to fight the Minotaur on the island of Crete. Before setting off, Theseus gave an offering to Apollo and returned victorious; thus, this celebration became a tradition to honor the god's help.

Pompaia – Pompaia honored Zeus and was an opportunity to ask him for good weather during colder months.[53]

Poseidea – Dedicated to Poseidon, this holiday was a time to honor the sea god and to ask for good weather during the winter storms.

Anthesteria – As one of four celebrations to Dionysus, Anthesteria welcomed the spring and everyone could come together, including everyday men and slaves.

Elaphebolion –Dedicated to Artemis, Elaphebolion was a time to make offerings to the huntress goddess, with cakes in the shapes of stags made of flour, honey, and sesame.

Laphria – Another celebration for Artemis, Laphria included offerings and sacrifices to the goddess, with a designated altar for the animal offerings.

Thargelia – Thargelia celebrated the birthdays of Artemis and Apollo and included animal and human (in earlier times) sacrifices to help with agricultural success. People brought offerings of the first fruits of the harvest to honor to the gods.

Skirophoria / Skira – Celebrated as the end of the year, Skirophoria had a procession out of Athens in honor of Athena to dissolve the year. This celebration included fasting, games, and the coming together of all social classes. This time included women feasting with each other and making their own sacrifices.

Attending Festivals & Ritual Celebrations

While festivals were instrumental in the daily life of ancient Greeks, not every ritual was open to everyone – especially women. Of the 120 days devoted to religious celebrations, most of the celebrations were intended to have only male participants.[54]

Women of the time were not allowed to vote, to own property, or to inherit. It was expected that women remained virgins until marriage and then had children and lived out their lives as mothers and wives. While texts might be incomplete and biased in these descriptions, the messaging toward women is seen in the description of goddesses too. Hera is shown as a vindictive wife, though Zeus had numerous affairs. Aphrodite is shown as an adulterer, though she was forced into a marriage she did not want. The 'ideal' woman seemed to be Penelope, the wife who waited for Odysseus to return from his journey. Or the Muses seemed ideal with their beauty and grace and were spoken of kindly and positively.

Only in Thesmophoria are women described as participating and having value. Made for citizen-wives, this festival celebrated Demeter and Persephone, and likely took place in October. Aligning with the agricultural season, this celebration retold the story of Kore (then Persephone) descending into the underworld to be with Hades. This was a time of year when harvests ended in Greece, as Demeter's grief for losing her daughter caused the lands to wither and die.

Women organized this ritual, and men were not allowed to know what had happened during the three days. It is suggested that the first day was dedicated to a sacrifice of piglets, the second day was reserved for fasting, and the last day was devoted to Demeter to ask for her to protect women's fertility.

> During festivals, in addition to sacrifices, hymns were sometimes sung. The standard structure was invocation of the god, honouring the god through recounting of one or more divine deeds, and finally a prayer for divine favour (Price 37).

Calling to the gods, creating space to recount their stories, and praying for their goodwill continues today in modern and reconstructionist practices.

Chapter 6
Greek Magic

> Magic is a difficult concept to identify in ancient Greece, because there was no category exactly equivalent to our modern notion. (The word *magos*, from which *magic* derives, referred to a Persian shaman.) It is likely that the use of what we might broadly describe as magical practices was widespread in all places and at all times, however. Although a number of Greek philosophers, including Plato and Aristotle, as well as members of the medical profession, tended to equate magic with fraud, there was never any systematic persecution of its practitioners (Garland 193).

It is wise to remember that magic today is not an easily defined term, nor is ritual something easily described. Like other features of society and religion, ancient Greece arrives in the present time in fragments and often without context. What is clear is that magic may not have been a widely used word, but it is a word that became a part of the retelling of this society's history.

You can see the use of magic in the myths. For example, Circe, the daughter of Helios, used her knowledge of herbs and potion-making to create liquids that turned men into pigs. Circe also helps Odysseus in his travels home by teaching him the magic of contacting the dead.

High Magic & Low Magic

Within Greek magic are two practices: Theurgy (***θεουργία***), or high magic, and Goetia (***γοητεία***), or low magic. Theurgy was magic to call on the gods to ask for their help and guidance. In this magic, one would call on the gods by invoking or evoking them, drawing them closer to becoming like the gods.

Also known as the divine work, theurgy is the participation between man and the gods.[55] To some, this is a formalized and liturgical practice, with certain things necessary to be aligned with 'actual' theurgy. There is debate about whether theurgy includes magical practices or 'just' communication with gods.

Goetia is lower magic, or magic not focused on the divine. The idea of Goetia related to fraudulent magic. This magic might include spells and witchcraft, often contained in books and grimoires. Author Owen Davies states that "magic was not distinct from religion but rather an unwelcome, improper expression of it – the religion of the other" when talking about the Roman view of magic.[56]

This differentiation speaks to the communal attitude of being in service to the whole versus the individual, even though the gods focused on their own desires and not on humans. However, as the gods were gods, they did not have the same rules. Perhaps it is wise to remember the words of Robert Parker in that:

> magic differs from religion as weeds differ from flowers, merely by negative social evaluation; magic was often seen as consisting of practices that range from silly superstition to the wicked and dangerous.[57]

And I would add that while it might seem easier to note these two magics as 'good' and 'bad' or 'white' and 'dark,' that is too simplistic.

Divination

While not everyone calls divination a practice of magic, the Greeks were interested in learning about the future (as already discussed in the section about oracles). There were both 'professional' and amateur diviners, priestesses and priests, and everyday people.

Some divination practices included:

Augury – The practice of noticing and interpreting omens.
Capnomancy – Looking at smoke for shapes that inform questions and curiosities.
Cledonomancy – Listening to conversations to overhear words that inform questions.
Cleromancy – Divining by throwing stones, dice, or lots.
Hydromancy – Interpreting the movements of water.
Necromancy – Consulting with the dead to gain wisdom.
Pyromancy – Looking into flames and fires for information.
Stikhomanteia – a.k.a. bibliomancy, the practice of gaining insight by looking at pieces of writing or books for random words and messages.
Thriai – Using pebbles to answer questions and predict future events.

Practitioners would also look at birthmarks, entrails, or birth membranes for shapes that contain messages that could be interpreted as divine messages.

Prayers

In keeping with the practice of theurgy, one turned to prayers as ways of connecting with deities. Walter Burkert, author of *Greek Religion,* notes a few things to keep in mind when praying to different gods. When praying to heavenly gods, one puts their arms up and palms upward to the sky. Prayers to underworld gods so not have arms stretched up, but rather downward with the words being whispered (Burkert 75).

Prayers require calling the name of the deity, telling their stories, reminding them of the good things you have done in their name, asking for what you want, and offering something in return for their support.[58]

There is also a message around prayers with deities about reciprocating effort. And this extends beyond the time of prayer. While Epicurus stated that the gods were not interested in the deeds of humans, Plato later noted that thinking the gods did not care about humans was an insult to the gods.

A person petitioning or praying to the gods must be a person who is doing good within their community. Not doing your part would be detrimental to the relationship with deities, and it is said the gods might lose interest in those who are not meeting their expectations in the relationship.

Spells

Shall we write about the things not to be spoken of?
Shall we divulge the things not to be divulged?
Shall we pronounce the things not to be pronounced?
Hymn to the Mother of the Gods,[59] Julian

The Greek Magical Papyri contained spells, including love potions, seeing the future, initiation, detecting thieves, invisibility, gaining friends, restraining anger, picking a plant, divining with Aphrodite, and more.

Love spells were designed to bring someone to you who was not already a lover. In a paraphrased description of a love spell, the one performing the spell took a seashell, wrote the names of holy beings on it with the blood of a black donkey, and recited words in a precise way. It is noted that the person doing the spell needed to be ready for quick results.[60] There are also specific symbols and words one could use to attract love.

And there are descriptions of how to invoke deities to help with affairs of the heart, including Selene or Aphrodite. One might also speak certain words over a special cup to entice the one they love.

One example of a memory spell in the *Greek Magical Papyri* describes the steps:

> Take hieratic papyrus and write the prescribed names with Hermaic myrrh ink. And once you have written them as they are prescribed, wash them off into spring water / from 7 springs and drink the water on an empty stomach for seven days while the moon is in the east. But drink a sufficient amount (Dieter Betz 9).

The spell describes what to write on the papyrus and the ingredients to include in the ink. I'm not including the full spell, as that is for you to find and use as you choose.

Curse Tablets & Amulets

Not all magic was practiced with positive intent. Some Greek magic practices were curses directed at specific people, often with a binding spell. As early as the fifth century BCE, there is evidence that curses were written onto lead tablets. These small tablets would be buried alongside the dead or near underworld cemeteries.[61]

The writing on the tablets could be straightforward, with the name of the one to be cursed and the name of the deity whose support was requested.[62] More often than not, the one who was petitioned for help was an underworld god. This magic would bind the subject of the curse from doing harm or taking an unwanted action. Christopher A. Farone notes that:

> Binding is one of the most popular weapons with which the gods fight each other in Greek myth: Cronus is bound by Zeus (Hes. Erga 173a); Zeus is threatened with the same fate at the hands of Poseidon, Apollo, and Hera (Il. 1.399-401); and Hephaestus binds Ares and Aphrodite in bed (Od. 8. 296 99), and even his own mother (Pindar, fr. 283 Snell; Plato, Rep. 378d). In part this phenomenon is a logical corollary to the fact of the gods' immortality; since they cannot kill one another, they can only defeat their enemies by imprisoning them, binding them, or similarly restricting their movements.[63]

There have also been charms (***kolossoi***) that one might compare to voodoo dolls, with needles placed at specific areas of the body for harm or arousal, depending on the intention of the magic. Amulets (phylacteries) protected the wearer from harm or sickness. Some amulets were created to help attract wanted energy (talismans).[64]

Magic could cause fear or worry in the hearts of everyday citizens, but it was also a tool for those who needed the help of the gods for their survival. Farmers needed good seasons for strong harvests. Those who were in danger required protection. Like many forms of magic, spells, and other practices were often borne of necessity. And many of the same or similar practices live into modern times.

Chapter 7

Taking It Home

I would say, some people are like constellations that only touch the earth for a season.

Circe, Madeline Miller

Having learned about the culture, the practices, and how magic and the gods were a part of everyday life, you might want to bring these practices into your life. Known as Hellenism, or the practice of carrying forward ancient Greek belief and worship, many non-Greeks have taken this practice of polytheism and animism into their lives and lands.

I was introduced to the Greek pantheon through interactions with specific gods, and my practice expanded with ongoing study. While some groups and organizations seek to bring precision to their magickal practice, I believe there is value and power in approaching the Greek gods from modern lenses too. After all, these are gods who want to be seen and known, and if they can be celebrated across time, then why not do so in other creative ways?

Reconstructionists work with the Greek gods by following the practices as outlined in texts, with words said in a certain manner and following specific steps (e.g., the way prayers should be structured). I encourage you to do what makes the most sense to you. I don't think there is one answer or one way. Find your way to say their names and walk in their stories. The best practice, in my opinion, is the one that keeps the gods alive.

How to Pray

If you go back to the section on prayers, you will see a specific outline of steps you can follow, according to Burkert's writing. In a 2018 blog called "Prayers of Ancient Greece," there is a list of prayers to inspire you. Here are a few that stand out to me:[65]

Dionysus: "O Lord, with whom Eros the subduer And the dark-eyed Nymphs And rosy Aphrodite Play, you who haunt The high mountain peaks, I beseech you, come to me With kind disposition, hear And fulfill my prayer (request here)." – Anacreon

Demeter: "Demeter, you who taught us to work the earth and provides for us so bountifully (your request here)." – The Iliad

The elements that are helpful to have in prayers to the Greek gods include:

- **Name** – Say and call out the name of the deity.
- **Epithets** – Most deities have epithets or titles associated with their name. These epithets describe aspects of the god, which might be more applicable to certain prayers. Some practitioners believe you must say all the epithets when calling a god. Or you might choose a few or just one, depending on the purpose of the prayer.
- **Praise and glory** – Just like humans, deities like to be praised. In a prayer, for example, you might recount a story of their bravery. Or you might speak of their physical qualities, e.g., Aphrodite's beauty and grace.
- **Request** – If you have a request to make in your prayer, include it after the god is honored. I encourage requests to be specific and flexible enough to hold multiple ways to be fulfilled. Better said, I don't tell the gods how to do what I ask, and I do ask for what I truly want and need.

- **Promise / oath / vow** – End a prayer with a commitment to reciprocation. This might include promising to give offerings or to act in a certain way to honor the god.

Putting this all together, it might look like this:

> Aphrodite Pandemos, Aphrodite Pandemos, Aphrodite Pandemos!
>
> You of beauty and kindness who walk with the people to hear their cries and know their hearts.
>
> I ask you to bless this community with love and compassion.
>
> And I promise to act in integrity during all conversations and interactions to show my commitment to love and compassion too.

Prayers need not be long or too detailed, and they can be as lengthy too. What is important is the honor you show to these deities and their power to help. Even more important is that when you promise something in return for a god's help, you need to follow through on that promise. While I don't believe gods care about human mistakes, I think any person you're in a relationship with should be able to trust your word. If your word is not trustworthy, what motivates a deity to help?

You might use prayers to start your days, including information about the god and how their energy might be supportive. You can use prayers for magical workings or holidays. You can also create prayers of celebration, as not all prayers need to ask for something.

Creating Temple Spaces

While you're not likely able to build a new temple for the Greek gods, you can create smaller temple spaces that honor their presence and make room for wonder. Small altars are a great way to create a designated spot for each god. These altars or rooms or spaces can include:

- Images, statues, or representations of the godd
- Items that correspond to the deity and help them recognize the altar as their space
- Place(s) for offerings, e.g., plate, cup, bowl, etc.
- Anything else that might aid in connecting to that god, e.g., a drum, a piece of jewelry dedicated to them, etc.

My experience has shown that each deity might want their own space, and that's not always possible. Instead, find a way to help the god feel seen and recognized. While I haven't encountered issues of gods sharing space with other gods, if you notice something doesn't feel quite right, move things around to see if that shifts the energy. I suggest a few basic practices:

Keep things tidy – You don't need to be overly organized to have a 'good' altar. And it is wise not to pile things up in one place. A practice I follow is to clean altars every six months or so. I remove the items, dust things off, remove things that need to be replaced, and update images or other items.

Provide fresh offerings – Whenever you can, keep the offerings on an altar fresh. Don't keep things on an altar when they are rotting, dying, or dried out unless that's part of your work. For example, I used to keep a small bowl of honey wine from Greece on my Aphrodite altar. This worked fine, but it also attracted bugs, so I would replace it with a fresh bowl if I noticed unexpected carcasses.

Spend time there – When you have an altar or temple space, spend time there. This space of collaboration and co-creation is enhanced by your participation. Do your reading about the gods there. Meditate or do spellwork there. Find ways to be in that space so your energies interact.

Change things as the relationship changes – As you get to know a god or change your relationships to deities, you might need to change the altar. There is no right or wrong to this, but it helps to change things to suit the emerging interactions. And these shifts help a deity feel seen and known.

You can create small temple spaces in nature or on a desk at work. These spaces don't need large or dramatic arrangements to be powerful. Focus instead on bringing honor to the god and the relationship you are building together.

Modern Offerings & Sacrifices

Offerings and sacrifices are a large part of Greek practices; thus, bringing those into your practice is a good idea too. I encourage you to think about how you might make a sacred commitment with these offerings. What might make a deity happy?

- Food
- Drink
- Water
- Flowers
- Honey
- Plants
- Small trinkets and treasures, e.g., a pearl necklace on an Aphrodite altar

Even beyond what you might include that would please a deity, think about what might be a sacrifice that requires a little more of you. This might be a journal of your feelings, a prayer you wrote, or a song you created in their honor. You might include offerings of your time by volunteering to support animals (for Artemis) or to clean up the local beach (Poseidon).

You don't need to kill things to make them appropriate offerings. Instead, think about what requires energy from you. And consider the intention behind each offering you make before you leave it on an altar.

Sacred Sites Today

Experiencing history helps me understand the land. Greece is a frequent site of pilgrimages because of excavations that uncovered many temples to the gods, as well as natural features that aligned with the beloved stories of Homer and Hesiod.

Acropolis – Located in Athens, the Acropolis is a visually stunning and nearly complete structure. This citadel sits on a rocky hill overlooking Athens and includes important sites, including the Parthenon, temples to Athena, sanctuaries for Zeus and Asclepius, and a theater for Dionysus. Pericles[66] led construction in the fifth century BCE, and while buildings were damaged during the war, many remain intact.

Mount Olympus – The highest mountain in Greece, Mount Olympus, is on the border of Macedonia and Thessaly and has more than 50 peaks, with the tallest peak being over 9500 feet. It was the first national park in Greece and is home to a diverse population of flora. Mount Olympus is near the city of Dion, which is dedicated to Zeus and the Olympians and is a sacred site.

Delos – This island near Mykonos is considered one of Greece's most important archaeological sites. Known as the birthplace of Artemis and Apollo, Delos has three sacred mounds, which may have honored Athena, and Mount Cynthus, which honored Zeus.

Knossos Palace – As one of the largest Minoan structures (more than 20,000 square meters), Knossos Palace is the setting for the myth of the labyrinth built by King Minos of Crete to protect them from the Minotaur before Theseus killed the creature.

Delphi – Once thought to be the center of the world by the Greeks, Delphi was the site of the oracles, or the sacred Pythia. People would travel here to seek guidance. The Delphi site includes temples for Athena and Apollo, the Sibyl rock (from which it is said the Pythia would deliver messages), a theater, a hippodrome, a sacred spring, and statues of athletes.

Mycenae – Mycenae was once a significant site in Greek civilization, showcasing examples of creativity and art, including the Lion Gate, Cyclopean Walls, tombs, and burial circles.

Troy – In Turkey, Troy was uncovered in the late 1800s, revealing multiple civilizations and settlements. The layers of the findings are labeled with Roman numerals to showcase the different ages, including the Neolithic, Early, Middle, and Late Bronze Ages, Dark Age, Classical and Hellenistic Ages, and Roman Age.

Petra tou Romiou / Aphrodite's Rock – On the shore of Cyprus is Aphrodite's Rock, where the goddess emerged from the water after the castration of Uranus.

Ancient Eleusis – Ancient Eleusis, a site dedicated to Demeter and Persephone (Kore), is where you can travel along a path and Processional Road to the temple of Demeter (Telesterion). The notable journey of Persephone to the Underworld was reenacted during a nine-day festival in September. People from surrounding areas would travel to the temple to be a part of the Eleusinian Mysteries, which showed Persephone's death and rebirth. During a famine in the 8th century BCE, the Greeks were told to bring sacrifices to Demeter's temple here.

Acheron – Also known as the Nekromanteion/Necromanteion, Acheron is the door to the Underworld, located on the north bank of the Acheron River. Also known as the oracle of the dead, visitors of Acheron were given a sparse diet to help them communicate with the dead. Travelers entered one door and left from another, instructed not to share what they had seen or learned.

Corinth – Once a large and thriving city, Corinth is home to the Temple to Apollo and a theater that can hold 15000 people.

When traveling to these sites, it is clear how the gods are revered and respected. From how these places are preserved to how they are restored; these places are not just locations but a part of history. While there are many temples, it is common for those who might want to practice magic or ritual to be stopped while visiting. Outsiders are not permitted to do things that seem related to witchcraft, paganism, etc., from what I am told by those who have traveled to these sites more recently. In any case, it is wise to check on the rules of engagement before setting foot in a place with a longer history than you.

Summing It Up

What I would recommend more than anything else is to read the stories of the deities and bring those stories into your everyday life. Consider the lessons to learn and how ancient Greece focused on the collective more than the individual. How can these gods show up every moment, not just when you need help?

Can you thank Hestia as you turn on the stove?
Can you remember Dionysus when you are laughing with friends?
Can you relate more to Zeus when you make boundaries to keep yourself safe?

You might reenact the gods' stories as a part of your practice and relationship-building, just as the mystery cults did for Demeter, Persephone, and Hades. Or how the cults of Dionysus acted out his travels across the lands.

Remember, the gods can be a part of every day, not just spells and rituals. When you can bring their stories and their wisdom into your life, these deities become the fabric that weaves a tapestry of resilience.

How can you bring the gods alive?

Part II

Chapter 8
Gods & Goddesses

> The world of Greek mythology was not a place of terror for the human spirit. It is true that the gods were disconcertingly incalculable. One could never tell where Zeus's thunderbolt would strike. Nevertheless, the whole divine company, with a very few and for the most part not important exceptions, were entrancingly beautiful with a human beauty, and nothing humanly beautiful is really terrifying. The early Greek mythologists transformed a world full of fear into a world full of beauty (Hamilton 11).

The heroes and beings of the Greek pantheon are many, so many it is difficult to include all of them in one place – perhaps literally and figuratively. These deities are vast and create a confusing family tree for those who try to make sense of the different interpretations of connections, births, and relations.

Theoi' (***Θεοί***) is the word for 'Gods' in Greek, and you will see this used with some god names to signify their positions as gods. Note too that there are Greek spellings for the names of the gods, as well as Roman names. More often, transliteration is used to phonetically spell the names of places and gods to better incorporate the original Greek letters. However, over time, certain spellings have become used more widely, making it seem confusing and inconsistent.

In my sources, there are variances, including discrepancies in pronunciations and spellings. I have tried to be consistent and accessible in the presentation of my research, but I imagine there are nuances I did not capture as well as I would have hoped. For some, this might seem messy; to me, this is exciting because it means there is no one answer. Instead, there is an opportunity to explore (seemingly) unending stories.

Primordial Gods

> *Tell me this from the beginning, Muses who dwell in Olympus, and say, what thing among them came first. First came the Chasm; and then the broad-breasted Earth, secure seat for ever of all the immortals who occupy the peak of snowy Olympus; the misty Tartara in a remote recess of the broad-pathed earth; and Eros, the most handsome among the immortal gods, dissolver of flesh, who overcomes the reason and purpose in the breasts of all gods and all men.*
>
> Theogony, Hesiod, p 6, translated by M. L. West

Here, we return to Theogony's first lines to learn of the beginning. A primordial[67] god is the oldest of deities. They arrived before the more commonly known and worshiped gods, and they existed more as forces or energies than forms. These gods were born of Gaia or born of themselves. Primordial, sometimes called primeval, gods were described in stories as human-bodied, but as the beginning of all, it is hard to contain their energies in that small form. This list could contain more beings, and this can serve as a starting point.

How I've formatted the names:

- The first word is a common name, which may or may not be transliteration.
- When separated into common name and transliteration, I use a '|'.

- Using '/' separates variations and aligns with the Greek spellings.
- Parentheses are used to enclose the Greek spelling(s).

***Aether* | / *Aithêr* (Αιθηρ)** – Mists of light filling the upper zones of air between heaven and earth.

***Ananke* | *Anankê* (Αναγκη)** – Energy of necessity, inevitability, and compulsion that circles creation; described as snake-like and partner of Chronos.

***Chaos* | *Khaos* / *Khaeos* (Χαος / Χαεος)** – Located between Aether and the earth's floor; birthed Erebus, Nyx, Aether, and Hemera.

***Chronos* | *Chronus* / *Khronos* (Χρονος)** – Self-created three-headed being (man, bull, lion) with a serpentine tail; related to time; also referred to as Aion/Aeon.

***Erebus* | *Erebos* (Ερεβος)** – Mists of darkness located on the journey to the underworld.

***Eros* (Ερος)** – Emerged during creation and enabled procreation; not to be confused with Aphrodite's son, Eros.

***Gaia* | *Gaia* / *Gaiê* / *Gê* / *Gaea* (Γαια / Γαιη / Γη)** – She birthed the universe; the body of the earth.

***Hemera* | *Hêmera* (Ημερα)** – She scattered the night to reveal Aether, her consort.

***Hydros* | *Hydros* (Υδρος)** – Being of water, and similar to Oceanus.

Nesoi* | *Nêsos / Nêsoi (Νησος / Νησοι) – Islands formed after being thrown into the sea when Poseidon broke them from the earth.

Nyx (Νυξ) – Night, often described as a woman in a star-covered mantle.

Ourea* | *Ouros / Oros / Ourea (Ουρεα / Ουρος / Ορος) Mountains born of Gaia during creation.

Phanes* | *Phanês (Φανης) – Creator god who came from a silver egg at the beginning of the universe.

Phusis* | *Phusis / Physis (Φυσις) – Another Mother Nature; related to Gaia and Tethys.

Pontus* | *Pontos (Ποντος) – Sea born of Gaia at the start of creation.

Tartarus* | *Tartaros (Ταρταρος) – Stormy pit below the earth's roots.

Thalassa (Θαλασσα) – Sea or the sea's surface, born of Aether and Hemera.

Thesis* | *Thesis / Thetis (Θεσις / Θετις) – Nurse for Mother Nature.

Uranus* | *Ouranos (Ουρανος) – Curve of heaven from horizon to horizon.

Gaia gave birth to Uranus before having children with him. But Uranus was upset with the Hecatoncheires they birthed, so he hid them, seeing them as monsters. Gaia was upset with this and asked her children to help punish their father. She created a sickle to castrate him, but Cronus (not the same as Chronos) was the only child willing to take on this task. Cronus castrated his father and became the leader of the Titans.

Titans

Earth bore first of all one equal to herself, starry Heaven, so that he should cover her all about, to be a secure seat for ever for the blessed gods; and she bore the long Mountains, pleasant haunts of the goddesses, the Nymphs who dwell in mountain glens; and she bore also the undraining Sea and its furious swell, not in union of love. But then, bedded with Heaven, she bore deep-swirling Oceanus, Koios and Kreios and Hyperion and Iapetos, Thea and Rhea and Themis and Memory, Phoebe of gold diadem, and lovely Tethys. After them the youngest was born, crooked-schemer Kronos, most fearsome of children, who loathed his lusty father. And again she bore the proud-hearted Cyclopes, Thunderer, Lightner, and Whitebolt stern of spirit.

Theogony, Hesiod, pp 6-7, translated by M. L. West

While the Olympians get most of the attention in Greek mythology, the Titans arrived after the primordial gods.

Coeus* | *Polos / Koios (Κοιος) – Child of Uranus and Gaia and husband of Phoebe, Coeus was instrumental in helping his siblings at the request of their mother. The God of Intellect was the Pillar of the North that held the Earth in place, and he held down the northern pole so he and his siblings could capture their father. He was also the god of heavenly oracles.

Crius / Krious* | *Kriōs / Kreios (Κριως / Κρειος) – The God of Constellations and child of Uranus and Gaia, Crius held down the south Pillar of the Earth to capture Uranus. Also known as

'The Ram,' he was the father of Astraios (Astraeus) and married Eurybia, daughter of the sea. His association with the south was important as it was the demarcation of the spring and the start of the Greek year.

Cronus* | *Kronos (Κρονος) – Cronus heeded his mother's call to castrate his father, Uranus. God of Time and associated with the sickle due to his actions, Cronus stepped into power over the Titans after overtaking his father. When Cronus then heard of a prophecy that his children would overthrow him, he swallowed his children when they were born, including Demeter, Hades, Hera, Hestia, and Poseidon. But Zeus was not swallowed, as his mother Rhea hid him away.

Hyperion (Υπεριων) – God of Heavenly Light, Hyperion married Theia, with whom he had several children, including Eos, Helios, and Selene. As the Pillar of the East, Hyperion helped capture Cronus.

Iapetus* | *Iapetos (Ιαπετος) – God of Mortality, Iapetus married Clymene and was father to Atlas. During the castration of Cronus, Iapetus was the fourth Pillar of the West, a role that Atlas held later. He fathered Prometheus and Epimetheus.

Mnemosyne (Μνημοσυνη) – Goddess of Memory, Mnemosyne invented words and language. It was her role to remember and memorize the stories of the gods. Mother of the Muses by Zeus, she was considered a minor Titan. Mnemosyne oversaw an underground oracle and may have been one of the Elder Muses.

Oceanus* | *Ōkeanos (Ωκεανος) – Oceanus was the freshwater river from which all other rivers flowed, and clouds emerged. Sometimes seen as a horned man with the tail of a fish instead of legs, he was married to Tethys and father of Potamoi, gods of rivers, and the Okeanides (Oceanids), nymphs of springs and fountains. Oceanus did not help in the castration of his father, Cronus, and did not participate in the War of the Titans.

***Phoebe* | *Phoibe* (Φοιβη)** – Goddess of the Oracle and Bright Intellect, Phoebe married Coeus and gave birth to Leto and Asteria. She was the third being to be the Oracle at Delphi and grandmother to Apollo, Artemis, and Hecate.

***Rhea* / *Rheia* | *Reia* / *Rea* (Ρεια / Ρεα)** – As the mother of gods and mountains, Rhea gave birth to Demeter, Hades, Hera, Hestia, Poseidon, and Zeus with Cronus. To protect her children from Cronus after he heard the prophecy of being overthrown by his children, Rhea took Zeus away, tricking Cronus by wrapping a stone in a blanket for him to swallow. She hid Zeus in a cave in Crete, protected by armed warriors. Rhea was seen with lions that pulled her chariot, wearing black-leaf robes and holding a scepter. Associated with the lion and hawk, Rhea was also found with silver fir that grew on local mountains. In her role, she was surrounded by attendants, including Pan, the goat-legged god.

***Tethys* (Τηθυς)** – Goddess of Fresh Water, Tethys brought nourishment to the world. Wife of Oceanus and mother of Potamoi (Rivers), the Okeanides/Oceanids (nymphs of springs, streams and fountains), and the Nephelai (Clouds), she was described as having a winged brow.

***Theia* (Θεια)** – Goddess of Sight and Prophesy, Theia married Hyperion and gave birth to Helios (Sun), Selene (Moon), and Eos (Dawn). She was associated with the blue sky.

***Themis* (Θεμις)** – Wife of Zeus and goddess of Law and Oracles, Themis watched over Delphi and gave the first laws to the gods to guide morality and justice. The word 'themis' is 'divine law,' so these laws were not for humans. As a wife of Zeus, Themis would counsel him on law.

They Might (Also) Be Titans?

With many translations and stories, gods can shift in terms of power and influence in the world of Greek mythology. The Titans listed before this section are the 12 most often named, but there are other beings. Like the minor Olympians, there might be minor Titans.

Arce / Árkē / Arke (Αρκη) – Daughter of Thaumas, this messenger goddess joined the Titans during the War of the Titans but was banished to Tartarus by Zeus and had her wings cut off after the Titans were defeated.

Asteria (Αστερια) – Asteria is the goddess of Night, Stars and Night Time Prophecy and mother of Hecate; possibly the same as Brizo. After the Titans lost, she was pursued by Zeus but leapt into the sea to escape him where she was transformed into the island of Delos.

Astraeus / Astraios (Αστραιος) – God of the Stars, the Winds, and Astrology, Astraeus fathered the four directional winds and the five wandering stars with Eos.

Atlas (Ατλας) – Atlas is the god of Astronomy who was captured by Zeus and punished by a sentence of carrying the weight of the world on his shoulders. He was later released and became a guardian of the pillars of the heavens.

Aura / Aurê (Αυρα / Αυρη) – Goddess of Breeze and Cool Morning Air, this virgin huntress was violated by Dionysus as a punishment for saying that Artemis could not be a virgin because Artemis' body was too womanly. Aura was turned into a stream by Zeus after going mad from the encounter with Dionysus and swallowing one of her twin sons whole.

Clymene* | *Klymenê / Klymene (Κλυμηνη) – One of the Okeanides and goddess of Fame who married Iapetus and mother of Prometheus and Atlas, Clymene was a handmaiden of Hera and played a role in the judgment of Paris as the personification of the gift Hera offered to Paris.

Cyclopes* | *Kyklôps / Kyklôpes (Κυκλωψ / Κυκλωπες) – Three one-eyed giants who assisted Zeus by crafting weapons for the gods to battle the Titans, including the lightning bolts for Zeus, a trident for Poseidon, and an invisible helm for Hades.

Dione* | *Diônê (Διωνη) – Known as the female version of Zeus, Dione was the mother of Aphrodite Pandemos by Zeus.

Eos* | *Êôs (Ηως) – Eos is the goddess of the Dawn who rose in the sky from Oceanus at the beginning of each day to scatter the darkness of night.

Epimetheus* | *Epimêtheus (Επιμηθευς) – God of Afterthought and Excuses, Epimetheus was the brother of Prometheus and tasked with filling the earth with men and animals. In doing so, he created more animals than men which led to Prometheus stealing fire to help mankind protect itself. This god married Pandora, despite being warned of her being created to cause troubles for humans.

Eurynome* | *Eyrynomē / Eurynomê (Ευρυνομη) – Sometimes referred to as an elder Okeanides and goddess of Water Meadows and Pastures, she married Zeus and gave birth to Kharities/Charities, or the Graces. In other sources, she was wife of Ophion who once ruled Olympus.

Hecate* | *Hekata (Ἑκατη / Ἑκατα) – The goddess of Magic and Necromancy is associated with torch-bearing Lampades (nymphs), demonic Lamiae (women heads/bodies and snake bodies), ghosts, and hell-hounds, she was one of three goddesses of the Eleusinian Mysteries.

Hecatoncheires* | *Hekatoncheir / Ekatoncheires (Ἑκατονχειρ / Ἑκατονχειρες) – Three immortal giants with 100 arms and 50 heads who assisted Zeus in the War of the Titans, they were later appointed as guards for the gates of Tartarus.

Helios* | *Hêlios / Helius (Ἡλιος) – Helios is the god of the Sun who rode across the sky in a chariot drawn by four fiery, winged steeds and possible father of Circe.

Lelantos* | *Lêlantos / Lelantus (Ληλαντος) – Known as the god of Air and Stalking during a hunt, Lelantos was the father of Aura.

Leto (Λητω) – Goddess of Motherhood and Protector of the Young who married Zeus, Leto gave birth to Artemis and Apollo.

Menoetius* | *Menoitios (Μενοιτιος) – This god of Force, Passion, and Ill Fate was struck by a thunderbolt of Zeus because of hubris.

Metis* | *Mêtis (Μητις) – The goddess of Counsel and Wisdom was one of the Okeanides who talked with Zeus during the War of the Titans. Metis was swallowed whole by her husband Zeus because of a prophecy that said she would bear a son more powerful than his father. Instead, she gave birth to Athena from her forehead, who emerged fully dressed in armor and arms.

***Ophion* | *Ophiôn* (Οφιων)** – The first king of heaven, Ophion was challenged by Cronus but was defeated and thrown into the ocean.

***Pallas* (Παλλας)** – This nymph and childhood companion of the goddess Athena was accidentally killed during their war games, Pallas was the father of Nike (Victory), Zelos (Rivalry), Kratos (Strength) and Bia (Power) by Styx.

***Perses* | *Persēs* / *Persaios* (Περσης / Περσαιος)** – God of Destruction who gave birth to Hecate, Perses was the source of the hot summer sun.

***Prometheus* / *Promêtheus* (Προμηθευς)** – As the god of Forethought and Counsel, Prometheus was tasked with creating man out of clay, but as he worked, he wanted to give man more than Zeus had instructed. Prometheus stole fire from the gods to give to man, hidden in a stalk of fennel, as man was not safe with all the animals created. As punishment, Zeus tasked Prometheus with creating Pandora, the first woman, to bring troubles to man. Prometheus was also arrested and tied to a stake on Mount Kaukasos/Caucasus where an eagle fed upon his liver, only for it to regenerate each day to be eaten again and again before Herakles/Herakles freed him.

***Selene* / *Selênê* (Σεληνη)** – Selene is the goddess of the Moon who rode sidesaddle on a horse or in a chariot led by a pair of winged steeds.

There are other gods who might be a part of the Titans, e.g., Tychon/Agathos, as there are conflicting stories that place some deities in some realms or who overlap with other deities while others might not be deities at all, but rather qualities of other deities.

Olympians

> The world of the ancient Greeks was full of deities: nymphs inhabited valleys and streams, Nereids lived in the depths of the sea, and satyrs roamed the woods. There were Titans, imprisoned deep in the bowels of the earth, and winged harpies, and sirens... This unruly multitude of gods was hard to manage, or even count, but the Greeks trusted that they all answered to Zeus, the supreme god, and to his immediate relatives who lived with him on Olympus... the gods of Olympus claimed the entire world as their own and demanded worship wherever they went: Homer, for example, described their travels all the way to Africa and northern Europe. It is partly because they were always conceived as universal powers that the gods of Olympus proved to be interesting to so many different people (Graziosi 5).

No matter how you learned of the Greek pantheon, it is likely you heard stories about the Olympians first. These are the 'major' deities, the ones who show up in story after story, who caused chaos and joy, and who inspired (and continue to inspire) movies, plays, stories, and poetry.

The Olympians won the war and took over from the Titans. And as in any power struggle, the struggle does not end with the conclusion of the battle. Whoever fights for power wants to stay in power, as stories and global history shows. These deities wanted the seats in Olympus, watching the humans as well as ensuring their power was always intact.

The number of Olympians varies, depending on interpretations of scholars and poets. In this book, we will cover the 13 gods who arrive in these lists most frequently. The goal is to give a basic familiarity with these gods by sharing some of their stories and describing their importance in the pantheon as well as in Greek mythology. But these are not complete histories.

I've listed the Olympians in alphabetical order for ease of reference. This is not a rank of importance or relevance. I note this specifically because Zeus, ruler of the gods, is listed last.

Aphrodite | Aphroditē (Ἀφροδίτη)

I will sing to lovely Aphrodite, revered goddess
crowned in gold, who protects the citadels of Cyprus,
island where the misty gales of Zephyros
cradled her in soft foam over the waves
of the roaring sea. The Horai, wearing gold tiaras,
gladly welcomed her, dressed her in divine robes,
placed on her immortal head a finely crafted crown
of lovely gold, set blossoms of mountain-copper
and costly gold in her pierced ears,
and adorned her soft throat and silvery breast
with gold necklaces like those that grace
the Horai wearing gold tiaras when they fly
to the gods' dance and their father's house.
When they had fully adorned her body,
they led her to the gods, who welcomed the sight
and offered her their hands. Each god prayed
to take her home as his wedded wife, so amazed
were they at the beauty of violet-crowned Cytheria.
Farewell, sweet gentle Goddess with dancing eyes:
grant me victory in this contest, ready my song –
but I will remember you and the rest of the song.

Homeric Hymn 6 to Aphrodite, translated by Diane J. Rayor

Aphrodite is the goddess of sensuality and beauty. In one story, she was born of sea foam from the severed genitals of

Uranus/Ouranos, arriving as the consequence of a fierce battle for power between the father, Uranus, and the son, Cronus. In the *Iliad*, she is born of Zeus and Dione. And in other stories, Aphrodite is said to have been born out of chaos or perhaps even born out of information that traveled with merchants from Asia Minor.

She is often relegated to stories related to jealousy of her beauty or the complexity of love, but Aphrodite is also a goddess of war. This is an important facet to remember as she was involved in the battle to become an Olympian and continued to be a fierce being through ongoing conflict.

Aphrodite married another Olympian, Hephaestus, for a while, but stories tell us that she was not interested in this marriage. After having been told to marry Hephaestus by Zeus as he didn't want other beings fighting over Aphrodite's beauty, she had affairs with Ares and others.

As a result of these affairs, Aphrodite eventually was no longer married to Hephaestus. (While the word 'divorce' isn't used, it's clear Hephaestus moved on to someone else.) While in the *Odyssey*, Aphrodite is said to be married to Hephaestus, in the *Iliad* and *Theogony*, Aphrodite was not married at all. In another telling of Aphrodite's story, Hephaestus tricked her into marrying him by asking Hera to sit on a golden throne he made. This magical chair trapped her until she agreed to let Hephaestus marry Aphrodite.

Select Attributes: Love, Beauty, Procreation, War, Sex, Pleasure.

Select Epithets: Kypris (of Cyprus), Philommeidês (Laughter Loving), Aphrogeneia (Foam Born), Khryseê (Golden), Eustephanos (Richly Crowned, Well Girdled), Ourania (Heavenly, Divine), Pandemos (Common, of the People), Praxis (Action), Symmakhia (Ally in Love), Migôntis (Union, Marriage), Morphô (Shapely Form), Areia (Warlike).

Select Symbols & Correspondences: Dove, Rose, Pomegranate, Myrtle, Girdle, Chariot, Sea Foam, Shellfish, Apple, Lettuce, Anemone (Flower), Pearl, Swine, Goose, Fishes.

Select Partners / Lovers: Hephaestus, Adonis, Ares, various shepherds.

Select Children: Eros, Harmonia, Erotes, Anteros, Himeros, Peitho, Priapos, Rhodos, Aeneas.

Notable Stories:

Psyche & Eros

In a certain city there lived a king and queen, who had three daughters of surpassing beauty. Though the elder two were extremely pleasing, still it was thought they were only worthy of mortal praise; but the youngest girl's looks were so delightful, so dazzling... Crowds of eager citizens, and visitors alike, drawn by tales of this peerless vision, stood dumbfounded, marvelling at her exceptional loveliness... and bowing their heads towards her in pious prayer as if she were truly the goddess Venus...

Day by day rumour gathered pace, and the fame of her beauty spread through the nearby islands, the mainland, and all but a few of the provinces. People journeyed from far countries... to witness the sight of the age. Venus's shrines in Paphos, Cnidos, and even Cythera itself were no longer their destinations. Her rites were neglected, her temples abandoned, her cushions were trodden underfoot, the ceremonies uncelebrated, the statues un-garlanded, the altars cold with forsaken ashes....

This extravagant bestowal of the honours due to heaven on a mere mortal girl roused Venus herself to violent anger. She shook her head impatiently, and uttered these words of indignation to herself with a groan: "Behold me, the primal mother of all that is, the source of the elements, the whole world's bountiful Venus, driven to divide my imperial honours with a lowly human! Is my name, established in heaven, to be traduced by earthly pollution? Am I to suffer the vagaries of vicarious reverence, a share in the worship of my divinity?... But she'll reap no joy from usurping my honours, whatever she may be: I'll soon make her regret that illicit beauty of hers."

The Golden Ass, Apuleius, Book IV: 28-31, translated by P.G. Walsh

Psyche was a beautiful girl, so beautiful that men sought her out and abandoned the temples of Aphrodite. Enraged, Aphrodite told her son, Eros, to find Psyche and make her fall in love with a hideous creature. But Eros fell in love with Psyche and decided to deceive her so they might be together. Eros disguised himself as an ugly creature who is a wonderful husband to Psyche, but she could only be with him at night. But as she couldn't see him and she promised not to look upon him, it was a lonely existence. Goaded by her sisters, Psyche decided to kill the horrible creature but saw his face and saw who he was. But Eros left when she saw him. To get her husband back, Psyche traveled to Aphrodite who realized what had happened and banished her son. In revenge, Aphrodite put Psyche through dangerous challenges until she fell into a deathly sleep after opening a box she was told not to open. Eros pleaded with Aphrodite to heal Psyche and to allow them to be married. Psyche was made immortal by Zeus and lived her life with Eros.

Trojan War

[At the wedding of Peleus and Thetis] Eris threw an apple in front of Hera, Athene, and Aphrodite as a prize for the most beautiful, and Zeus instructed Hermes to take them to

Alexander on Mount Ida, to be judged by him for their beauty. They promised to give Alexander gifts; Hera promised him universal dominion if she were preferred above all other women, while Athene offered victory in war, and Aphrodite the hand of Helen. He decided in favor of Aphrodite, and sailed to Sparta.

The Library of Greek Mythology, Apollodorus, Epit. 3.2, translated by Robin Hard

Because Aphrodite allowed Paris to take Helen of Troy away, it is said that the goddess of love started the Trojan War. Eris, a being of discord, offered a golden apple to the most beautiful goddess during a wedding celebration. Hera, Athena, and Aphrodite all vied for this apple. While Hera and Athena offered Paris power, Aphrodite offered him the hand of the most beautiful woman, Helen. Paris decided to marry Helen, winning Aphrodite the apple. As Helen was already married to Menelaus, this contest started the war between the Greeks and the Trojans.

Apollo | Apollōn (Aπoλλων)

Phoibos, even the swan wings a high song to you
as it alights on the riverbank of the swirling Peneios.
The sweet-sounding bard, with lyre pitched
high and clear, always sings of you first and last.
And so farewell, Lord, as I appease you with song.

Homeric Hymn 21 to Apollo, translated by Diane J. Rayor

Apollo is an Olympian of healing, song, poetry, and prophesy. The twin brother of Artemis, he is associated with archery and hunting. Youthful in appearance, Apollo is beard-less and long-haired. He has many lovers, as well as being one who can shapeshift.

A child of Zeus and Leto, Apollo was born into the world while being hidden from Hera. Zeus was well-known for his affairs outside of his marriage, and Leto's affair with Zeus resulted in Artemis and Apollo's birth. Hera chased after Leto, threatening her with death. Eventually Leto found a place to give birth, the island of Delos, where she birthed Artemis first who helped to birth her brother.

While Apollo is seen as a healer, he is also a protector who helps ward off evil. People would go to Apollo to ask for healing during times of illness, often pleading for his support and guidance. Apollo was the deity to visit and give offerings to when an illness had been healed. Some would offer songs in Apollo's name during healings. At the same time, Apollo's arrows are associated with bringing disease and death to people. As Apollo could bring misery into the lands, followers would offer large sacrifices to avoid plagues and other misfortunes.

Many writings about Apollo speak of him as being the most Greek, or Hellenistic, of the Olympian gods. Apollo's association with the sun is the association that places him in the 'most Greek' distinction, as the sun was an important symbol for the Greek people, encapsulating their identity and the culture.

Apollo was known as a lover of all genders, taking on many lovers during his lifetime.[68] In some retellings, he is seen as a queer deity, taking on Orion as a lover a retelling of the story of Artemis and Orion.[69] But in his protectiveness of his twin sister, Apollo sent a scorpion into the dreams of Orion to kill him. Orion escaped, but fled into the ocean, only to be killed by Artemis after an intentional miscommunication, spurned by Apollo.

While Apollo is a complicated being, his presence enables an ongoing understanding of relationship, loyalty, healing, and prophesy.

Select Attributes: Healing, Music, Dance, Archery, Prophesy, Poetry, Sun.

Select Epithets: Phoibos / Phoebus (Bright), Thearios (of the Oracle), Agraios (of the Hunt), Paian (Healer), Alexikakos (Averter of Evil or Harm), Epikourios (Helping), Pythios (Pythian), Delphios (of Delphi), Meliai (of the Ash Trees), Aktaois (of the Coast), Patrôios (of the fathers), Thermios (of Lupine flowers), Aiglêtos (Shining), Horios (Boundaries and Borders).

Select Symbols & Correspondences: Bow and Arrow, Lyre, Raven, Rays of Light, Laurel Branches, Swan.

Select Partners / Lovers: Hecate, Hestia, Calliope, Mousai, Ourania, Thalia, Daphne, Kyrene, Aria, Hecuba, Kassandra, Phthia, Adonis, Hykinthos, Hymenaios, Kyparissos, Koronis, Kreusa, Khrysorthe, Calliope, Orion.

Select Children: Aristaios, Asklepios, Ion, Koronos, Apis, Linos, Delphos, Philammon, Amphissos, Orpheus, Miletos, Scylla.

Notable Stories:

Saving Leto

> *And in it was wrought Phoebus Apollo, a stripling not yet grown up, in the act of shooting at mighty Tityos who was boldly dragging his mother by her veil, Tityos whom glorious Elate bare, but Earth nursed him and gave him second birth.*
>
> Argonautica, Apollonius Rhodius, Book 1, translated by R.C. Seaton

Apollo's birth was a dramatic adventure, but Leto was able to give birth to her twins, Hera continued to be upset with Leto for this. In one story, Leto traveled to Delphi, where Hera told the giant, Tityos, to abduct Leto. However, Apollo saved his mother by slaying the giant with arrows. Other versions state that Artemis may have been the slayer of the giant too.

Python Slaying

Hera bore Typhon, unlike a god or a human,
clever, awful and cruel, a bane for mortal folk.
At once, cow-eyed Queen Hera brought
evil to evil and the she-dragon welcomed him –
Typhon did much harm to the glorious human race.

Whoever met the she-dragon died that day,
until Lord Apollo, who works from afar,
shot her with a piercing arrow – she lay down, shattered
with brutal pain, wheezing heavily, thrashing on the ground.

Homeric Hymn 3 to Apollo, 351-359, translated by Diane J. Rayor

To guard the oracle of Delphi, Gaia sent a monstrous dragon-like serpent, Python, to the temple. As Apollo was told he was the guardian of the temple, he sent hundreds of arrows to Python, in the hopes of slaying it. When Apollo succeeded, the oracle was named Pythian for the python corpse left by Apollo's arrows. Some stories say Leto was pursued by a serpent during her pregnancy with Apollo and Artemis, which may have encouraged Apollo to take revenge on Python.

Ares | Arēs (Αρης)

Mighty Ares, gold-helmed chariot master,
shield-bearer, bronze-armored city guard, strong-willed,
strong-armed, untiring spear strength, defense of Olympos,
father of Victory in war, aid to Themis,
tyrant to enemies, leader of righteous men,
wielding manhood's scepter, your red orb whirling
among the seven paths of the planets through the ether
where your fiery stallions bear you above the third orbit.

Hear me, ally of mortals, you grant blossoming youth,
blazing down a soft flame into my life
and warrior strength that I might drive
bitter wickedness from my head,
my mind bending my soul's deceitful impulse,
to restrain my heart's sharp temper provoking me
to enter bone-cold battle. But you, Blessed One,
give me courage to stay within the gentle laws of peace,
fleeing enemy battle and violent death.

Homeric Hymn 8 to Ares, translated by Diane J. Rayor

Ares is quickly and consistently associated with war. With his Roman counterpart as Mars, he is seen as being always dressed for battle. Often, he wears armor and a helmet, carrying a shield and sword, while also described as being nude. Other descriptions of Ares show him as a more mature being, while some stories speak of his youthfulness.

Born to Zeus and Hera, Ares was a sibling or half sibling of Athena, Aphrodite, Apollo, Artemis, Hermes, Dionysus, and Hephaestus. Ares was one of Aphrodite's lovers, caught in a net by Hephaestus when he discovered their affair. The affair itself caused Ares to be temporarily banished from Olympus. During his time with Aphrodite, they had several children, including Deimos (Fear), Phobos (Terror), and Harmonia (Peace).

During the Trojan War, the Olympians were divided in who they supported, with Ares being a part of the group that supported the Trojans instead of the Greeks. Ares is portrayed as being violent, ungovernable, and terrifying. He was willing to kill and to go into battles for the love of fighting. At the same time, Ares is described as the most human of all the Olympians.

The worship of Ares was not widespread in Greece, as he was not seen as a popular deity. But his presence was necessary as wars and fighting were common in ancient Greece.

Select Attributes: War, Battle, Armed, Bloodthirsty, Courage, Revenge.

Select Epithets: Thêritas (Beastly), Hippios (of Horses), Aphneios (Abundant), Gynaikothoinas (Feasted by Women), Miaiphonoes (Blood-stained), Andreiphontês (Destroyer of Men), Khalkokorustês (Armed with Bronze), Enkhespalos (Spear-brandishing), Enyalios (Warlike), Deinos (Fearsome), Oxus (Sharp, Piercing).

Select Symbols & Correspondences: Warrior Helm, Sword, Spear, Serpent, Moon.

Select Partners / Lovers: Aphrodite, Eris, Aerope, Kyrene, Asterie, Otrere, Ilia, Astyoche, Demonice, Eos, Persephone, Phylonome.

Select Children: Anteros, Deimos, Enyalios, Eros, Harmonia, Kyknos, Nike, Phobos, Amazones, Diomedes, Hippolyte, Romulus.

Notable Stories:

Jealousy of Adonis

With calm face ever-smiling Aphrodite rang out her unfailing laugh, when she saw the birthday games of the happy beasts. She turned her round eyes delighted in all directions; only the boars she would not watch in their pleasures, for being a prophet she knew, that in the shape of a wild boar, Ares with jagged tusk and spitting deadly poison was destined to weave fate for Adonis in jealous madness.

Dionysiaca, Nonnus, 41.194, translated by William Henry Denham Rouse

While Ares and Aphrodite were lovers, Aphrodite did not limit her partners. She found herself captivated by Adonis, a beautiful man who captured the hearts of everyone who saw him. Aphrodite was so distracted by him that neglected her duties. Ares became jealous of Aphrodite's obsession, so Aphrodite sent Adonis to live with Persephone in the underworld, away from her and away from others who might fall in love with him. One time, Aphrodite had to travel and left Adonis in the forest to hunt as he liked. But she warned him to stay away from any animal or beast that did not run from him. During his time in the woods, Adonis was attacked by a wild boar, Ares in disguise, and died as Aphrodite returned upon hearing his screams. As Persephone was also in love with Adonis, she and Aphrodite decided to have Adonis stay with each of them for four months of the year, with the other four months being for Adonis to spend alone.

Battle with Herakles

Though they were brothers, these were not of one spirit; for one was weaker but the other a far better man, one terrible and strong, the mighty Herakles. She bore him through the embrace

of the son of Cronos lord of dark clouds and the other, Iphicles, of Amphitryon the spear-wielder – offspring distinct, this one of union with a mortal man, but that other of union with Zeus, leader of all the gods. And he slew Cycnus, the gallant son of Ares. For he found him in the precinct of far-shooting Apollo, him and his father Ares, never sated with war. Their armour shone like a flame of blazing fire as they two stood in their chariot: their swift horses struck the earth and pawed it with their hoofs, and the dust rose like smoke about them, pounded by the chariot wheels and the horses' hoofs, while the well-made chariot and its rails rattled around them as the horses plunged. And blameless Cycnus was glad, for he hoped to slay the warlike son of Zeus and his charioteer with the sword, and to strip off their splendid armour. But Phoebus Apollo would not listen to his vaunts, for he himself had stirred up mighty Heracles against him. And all the grove and altar of Pagasaean Apollo flamed because of the dread god and because of his arms; for his eyes flashed as with fire. What mortal man would have dared to meet him face to face save Heracles and glorious Iolaus?

Shield of Heracles, Hesiod, 50 – 74, translated by H.G. Evelyn-White

One of Ares' sons, Kyknos, took after his father and murdered visitors on their way to the oracle at Delphi. In one version of the story, this situation angered Apollo who sent Herakles to kill Kyknos, which upset Ares. While Ares tried to retaliate and fight for his son, he was unsuccessful as Herakles was protected by Athena and couldn't be harmed. During the fight, however, Ares was injured by Herakles.

Artemis (Αϱτεμις)

Sing, Muse, to Artemis, sister of the Far-shooter,
virgin who rains arrows, raised with Apollo.

After watering her horses along the rushes of Meles,
she swiftly drives her golden chariot through Smyrna
to vine-laden Klaros where Silverbow Apollo,
who strikes from afar, awaits the one who rains arrows.
You and all the goddesses, rejoice in my song:
I begin first to sing about you and yours –
having begun with you, I will turn to the rest of the hymn.

Homeric Hymn 9 to Artemis, translated by Diane J. Rayor

Artemis, the huntress with a bow and arrow, traveled through the forests and mountains with her hounds. The twin sister of Apollo, and born of Zeus and Leto, Artemis was a chaste goddess who wanted only to hunt and to be in nature. As a child, she asked her father for a bow and arrow and permission to hold onto her maidenhood and freedom from marriage. The young Artemis also asked for 80 attendants to be part of her retinue, to sing and dance with her in the woods.

There are various interpretations of the virginity of Artemis. To some, this meant she was a virgin, but to others, this meant she was not married or bound to any one person. As a virgin goddess, Artemis attended childbirths and helped mothers during difficult labors, just as she had done for Leto when birthing Apollo.

Artemis was well-revered with many temples for her in and around Greece. It was also common to hear stories of her killing anyone who looked upon her or threatened her virginity. Some translations will describe how Artemis is able to hit anything she shoots. Artemis is proud of her hunting and not pleased by anyone who proclaims to be better than her. At the same time, she was a fierce protector of young girls and their chastity and called upon during rites of passage into womanhood.

Often pictured as a younger deity, Artemis is described as tall with a headband adorned with a crescent moon.

Select Attributes: Hunt, Animals, Birth, Nature / Life Cycles, Death, Health, Dance, Song.

Select Epithets: Pôtnia Therôn (Queen of Beasts), Iokheaira (of Showering Arrows), Hekatê (Far Shooting), Agrotera (of the Hunt, Huntress), Thêroskopos (Hunter of Wild Beasts), Keladeinos (Strong Voiced), Hagnê (Chaste, Purity).

Select Symbols & Correspondences: Bow and Arrows, Crescent Moon, Deer, Bear, Spear, Amaranth, Torch, Lyre, Hounds, Mugwort (Artemisia).

Select Partners / Lovers: none

Select Children: none

Notable Stories:

War of the Titans

> *After Juno [Hera] saw that Epaphus, born of a concubine, ruled such a great kingdom, she saw to it that he should be killed while hunting, and encouraged the Titanes to drive Jove [Zeus] from the kingdom and restore it to Saturnus [Cronus]. When they tried to mount heaven, Jove [Zeus] with the help of Minerva [Athena], Apollo, and Diana [Artemis], cast them headlong into Tartarus.*
>
> Fabulae from The Myths of Hyginus, Hyginus, 150, translated by Mary Grant

During the War of the Titans, Agamemnon, the king of Mycenae, boasted he was a better hunter than Artemis after killing a sacred stag. Furious, Artemis sent strong winds to prevent his boat from sailing. The men made a sacrifice of a young girl to

Artemis in return for their actions. But Artemis saved the young girl, Iphigeneia, and made her immortal, leaving a deer in the girl's place.

Artemis & Persephone

[Zeus] bade him [Haides] seize her [Persephone] as she was gathering flowers on Mount Etna, which is in Sicily. While Proserpina was gathering flowers with Venus [Aphrodite], Diana [Artemis], and Minerva [Athena], Pluto [Haides] came in his four-horse chariot, and seized her.

Fabulae from The Myths of Hyginus, 146, Hyginus, translated by Mary Grant

When the young Persephone (Kore) picked flowers in a field with Artemis, Aphrodite, and Athena, according to some stories, Kore was stolen by Hades, as directed by Zeus (or possibly Gaia). Artemis is also said to have been present during the search for Kore in the underworld by her mother, Demeter, perhaps becoming a Chthonian (Underworld) goddess for her efforts in moving between the worlds.

Athena | Athēnē (Αθηνη)

I sing of the glorious goddess Pallas Athena,
owl-eyed deity with crafty wisdom and steady heart,
revered virgin, stalwart guardian of the city,
Tritogeneia. From his august head, cunning Zeus
himself gave birth to her, born in warlike armor
of gleaming gold. Awe seized all the gods watching.
She sprang quickly from his immortal head
and stood in front of Zeus who bears the aegis,
shaking her sharp spear. Great Olympos reeled
violently beneath the might of her shining eyes,

the earth let out an awful cry, and the deep shifted,
churning with purple waves. Suddenly the sea
held still and the shining son of Hyperion halted
his swift horses a long while until the maiden
Pallas Athena lifted the godlike armor
from her divine shoulders, and wise Zeus rejoiced.
Hail, child of aegis-bearing Zeus –
but I will remember you and the rest of the song.

Homeric Hymn 28 to Athena, translated by Diane J. Rayor

Athena was born under unusual circumstances, which heralded her place among the Olympians. Gaia and Uranus told Zeus that since he had laid with Metis who would birth a strong warrior, he should swallow his lover whole in case she birthed something stronger than he was. However, Athena was later born from the forehead of Metis, fully formed and ready for battle.

This goddess is closely connected with the idea of talent and skill-building and gaining wisdom through practice and action. Known for weaving, Athena is associated with crafts and pottery during peacetimes.

Athena may have started as a more domestic goddess before warrior aspects and attributes were added. But she is a war goddess, as depicted in art and stories. Wearing a protective breastplate and helmet, she is always ready for battle. Likely the inspiration for the city being named Athens, Athena led soldiers into battle and fought alongside them. She was described in *The Odyssey* as being a close advisor of Odysseus during his journeys.

Known as a virgin goddess, Athena does not have lovers or partners. Much like Artemis, she stands alone in her power and agency. This might be why she has a single owl for a companion, or why some believe Athena was a wise owl and not human-like.

Select Attributes: Wisdom, Crafts, Weaving, War, Chastity, Defending of Cities, Peace.

Select Epithets: Nikê (Victory), Areia (of War, Warlike), Sthenias (of Strength), Sôteira (Savior), Eryma (Defender), Polioukhos (City Protector), Hygeia (of Good Health), Apatouria (of Deception), Oxyderkês (Sharp Sighted), Koryphagenês (Born of the Head), Parthenos (Virgin, Maiden), Xenia (f Hospitality), Kyparissia (of the Cypress Grove), Axiopoinos (Returning Vengeance), Polias/Pallas (of the City).

Select Symbols & Correspondences: Owl, Snake, Olive Tree, Gorgoneion (amulet with a Gorgon head), Aigis (Snake-Trimmed Cape), Aegis (shield or breastplate).

Select Partners / Lovers: none

Select Children: none

Notable Stories:

Athena and Arachne

> *Pallas [Athena] could not blame that work, nor could Envy censure it. The yellow-haired Virgin grieved at her success, and tore the web embroidered with the criminal acts of the Gods of heaven. And as she was holding her shuttle made of boxwood from Mount Cytorus, three or four times did she strike the forehead of Arachne, the daughter of Idmon. The unhappy creature could not endure it; and being of a high spirit, she tied up her throat in a halter. Pallas, taking compassion, bore her up as she hung; and thus she said: "Live on indeed, wicked one, but still hang; and let the same decree of punishment be pronounced against thy race, and against thy latest posterity,*

that thou mayst not be free from care in time to come." After that, as she departed, she sprinkled her with the juices of an Hecatean herb.

Metamorphoses, Ovid, 6.1 ff, translated by Henry Thomas Riley[70]

Arachne was a human whose weaving abilities were said to rival those of Athena. In some stories, Arachne was humble with her gift, but in others, she challenged Athena. In a competition, Athena and Arachne wove separate pieces, with Athena weaving a tapestry of the brilliance of the gods, while Arachne wove a tapestry that showed the love affairs of the gods. When the weaving was done, it was clear that Arachne's skills were superior, which angered Athena. Athena was so upset she tore the tapestry into pieces, which upset Arachne, who hung herself with the torn pieces. But Athena pitied Arachne and saved her by loosening the strands and turning Arachne into a spider.

Madness of Ajax

When Achilles' armour was offered as a prize to the bravest, Aias [Ajax] and Odysseus entered the lists. With the Trojans acting as judges, or according to some, the allies, Odysseus was picked as the winner. Aias was so overcome by resentment that he planned a night attack on the army; but Athene [Athena] drove him out of his wits and turned him against the cattle, sword in hand, and in his delusion, he slaughtered the cattle along with their herdsmen, supposing them to be Achaeans. Afterwards, however, when he had recovered his wits, Aias killed himself.

The Library of Greek Mythology, Apollodorus, Epit. 5.6, translated by Robin Hard

Ajax was upset to lose a competition to Odysseus and decided to attack Odysseus' army. Athena caught word of this plan and placed madness on Ajax so he would think he was in battle, while he was killing cattle and their herdsmen. When Ajax realized what he had done, he killed himself.

Demeter | Dēmētēr (Δημητηρ)

I sing of the revered goddess, rich-haired Demeter,
and her slim-ankled daughter, whom Hades snatched
(far-seeing, thundering Zeus gave her away)
while she and Ocean's deep-breasted daughters played,
far from golden blade Demeter, who bears shining fruit.
She picked lush meadow flowers: roses, crocuses,
lovely violets, irises, hyacinths – and a narcissus
Gaia grew as a lure for the blossoming girl,
following Zeus' bidding, to please Lord of the Dead.
Everyone marveled at the bewitching sight,
immortal gods and mortal folk alike:
from its root bloomed a hundred sweetly
scented heads, and all wide heaven above,
all earth, and the salty swell of the sea laughed.
Amazed, she stretched out both hands to pick
the charming bloom – and a chasm opened
in the Nysian plain. Out sprang Lord of the Dead,
god of many names, on his immortal horses.

Homeric Hymn 2 to Demeter, 1-18, translated by Diane J. Rayor

Demeter, mother of Persephone (Kore), is an Olympian whose power and reverence has grown over time. While Hestia started in roles Demeter now takes up, Demeter grew into a more widely worshiped deity. Gaia played a prominent role amongst the gods before Demeter became a more central figure to the everyday Greeks because Demeter seemed to have more of a detailed personality than Gaia. Responsible for the seasons of growth, Demeter's role in everyday lives was central and celebrated.

Born of Cronus and Rhea, Demeter gave birth to Persephone with Zeus. Sometimes named Kore as a child, Persephone was taken or traveled to the underworld (depending on the story) without her mother knowing, causing Demeter to grieve and rage until she found her daughter again. Pictured in a dark cloak with blonde hair, Demeter is seen traveling the earth to find her child.

Like her siblings, Demeter was swallowed by Cronus to prevent his offspring from taking his power from him. But since Zeus was not swallowed, she was eventually freed and born again.

Demeter is an underworld goddess; one you might present a sacrifice to upon the death of a loved one if you lived in Sparta. It was thought a sacrifice helped souls in moving from their earthly lives into the underworld with ease.

The conflation of Demeter with Rhea and Gaia can present confusion, as they were distinct from each other during earlier periods. But as time progressed, these goddesses have merged into less distinct energies, however, they can be celebrated in their unique stories which serve to demonstrate their individuality.

Select Attributes: Grain, Agriculture, Law & Order, Mysteries of the Afterlife, Fertility of the Earth.

Select Epithets: Khthonia (of the Earth), Ploutodoteira (Giver of Wealth), Megala Thea (Great Goddess), Thesmophoros (Bringer of Law), Prostasia (Patron, Leader), Eleusinia (of Eleusis), Pylaiê (of the Gates), Erinys (Fury, Wrath), Hôrêphoros

(Bringer of Seasons), Aglaodôros (Bestower of Splendid Gifts), Kallistephanos (Beautiful Crowned), Kyanopeplos (Dark Veiled, Cloaked), Hagnê (Pure, Chaste), Potnia Theaôn (Queen Amongst Goddesses), Mystêria (Mysteries).

Select Symbols & Correspondences: Wheat, Cornucopia, Winged Serpent, Torch.

Select Partners / Lovers: Zeus, Iasion, Poseidon, Karmanor.

Select Children: Persephone (Kore), Ploutos, Philomelos, Korybas, Areion, Despoine, Eubouleus, Khrysothemis.

Notable Stories:

Search for Persephone

Snatching the unwilling girl [Persephone], he [Hades] carried her off
in his golden chariot, as she cried and screamed aloud
calling to her father, son of Kronos, highest and best.
None of the immortal gods or mortal folk
heard her cry, nor the Olives shining with fruit –
except the daughter of Perses, tender-hearted
Hekate, veiled in light, heard from her cave
and Lord Helios, Hyperion's shining son,
heard the girl calling to her father, son of Kronos.
Zeus sat far away from the gods, in his temple echoing
with prayers, accepting rich offerings from mortals.
But her father's brother, Kronos' son of many names,
Lord of the Many Dead, stole the unwilling girl
away on his immortal horses, with a nod from Zeus.

Homeric Hymn 2 to Demeter, 19-32, translated by Diane J. Rayor

Demeter was grief-stricken by the disappearance of Persephone (Kore). Demeter turned and suddenly found her daughter gone. When this happened, Demeter asked everyone she could think of where Persephone had gone. She asked the gods, she asked humans, and she traveled over the lands to find her daughter. In her grief, Demeter traveled for nine days, almost giving up. But Hecate arrived with news that she had heard Persephone's voice, and that spurned Demeter to continue her search. In her grief, Demeter left the earth barren and the fields dying. In some tales, Demeter became angry and pleaded with the gods to help her find Persephone. And in her rage, she continued to ignore her duties, focusing instead on the ongoing search. In other accounts, Demeter dressed like a human woman and became a nursemaid. But Iris found Demeter and tried to talk her out of her absence as instructed by Zeus, because the fields were dying, and people were starving. Demeter refused this request and Zeus talked Hades into releasing Persephone back to her mother, but as Persephone had already eaten food in the underworld, she would need to stay for part of the year and would return to her mother the other part of the year.

The Sirens

> *The Sirens, daughter of the River Achelous and the Muse Melpomene, wandering away after the rape of Proserpina [Persephone], came to the land of Apollo, and there were made flying creatures by the will of Ceres [Demeter] because they had not brought help to her daughter. It was predicted that they would live only until someone who heard their singing would pass by.*
>
> Fabulae from The Myths of Hyginus, 141, Hyginus, translated by Mary Grant

The Nymphai/Nymphae were once servants of Demeter and handmaids to Persephone. When Persephone went missing, some stories say these servants did not help Demeter, while other stories describe them helping. As a result, Demeter turned the Nymphai into the Sirens, bird-shaped monsters who call men to their deaths. This transformation is seen as either a curse or a blessing.

Dionysus | Dionysos (Διονυσος)

I sing of ivy-crowned Dionysos, the roaring god,
radiant son of Zeus and glorious Semele.
Lovely nymphs, receiving him from his lord father,
nursed him at their breasts and fostered him tenderly
in the Nysian valleys. He grew up in a fragrant cave,
by his father's will, counted among the immortals.
When the goddesses had raised him, a god celebrated
in so many hymns, he roamed through forest haunts,
draped with ivy and laurel. The nymphs followed
as he led the way: their loud cry filled the vast forest.
Rejoice, Dionysos, god of the plentiful grape!
May we come again rejoicing to this season
And from that season on, through the revolving years.

Homeric Hymn 26 to Dionysus, translated by Diane J. Rayor

Dionysus is a well-known Olympian god, easily recognized by the drunken revelry associated with him. He is a wild deity surrounded by those who worship him, demonstrating their commitment and devotion with frenzied dancing. Sometimes a youthful god, he is also described as being older with a beard.

Born of Zeus and Semele,[71] or of Zeus and Dione, or of Zeus and Selene, or even a child of Persephone, Dionysus was twice-born after Hera tricked the then-pregnant Semele into having Zeus stand before her in his godly power. Semele was consumed by his lightning bolts when Zeus arrived. Realizing Hera's ploy, Zeus took his son into his thigh to be safe until birth.

While Dionysus is often found in the Olympians, some stories show he was not always a part of this group. At first, Hestia was included in the Olympians, but resigned her seat as she did not want to be a part of her siblings' ongoing drama, as it was not in her peaceful nature. In this stepping down, Dionysus took her seat. Other accounts say Dionysus was brought to Olympus with Hephaestus.

Surrounded by satyrs and maenads, Dionysus is seen in *The Bacchae,* a celebrated play by Euripides, taking revenge on King Pentheus for killing his aunts. The title of the play is linked to the name of women dedicated to Dionysus and who rip the king to pieces for his deeds, as well as for the king's acceptance of the rumor that Dionysus was not born of Zeus.

Select Attributes: Winemaking, Festiveness, Ecstasy, Wild Abandon.

Select Epithets: Bakkhos (of Bacchic Frenzy), Bromios (Noisy, Boisterous), Mainolês (Mad), Nyktelios (of the Night), Hestiôs (Of the Feast), Androgynos (Androgynous), Staphylitês (of the Grape), Lênaios (of the Wine Press), Theoinos (God of Wine), Kissios (of the Ivy), Taurophagos (Bull Eater), Eleuthereus (of Liberation), Sôtêrios (Recovery from Madness), Patrôios (Paternal).

Select Symbols & Correspondences: Thyrsus (pine cone staff), Bull, Serpent, Grapevine, Ivy, Vines, Plays, Song, Queerness, Vegetation, Panther.

Select Partners / Lovers: Ariadne, Aphrodite, Khione, Aura, Hera, Nikaia, Kronois.

Select Children: Priapos, Methe, Thysa, Telete, Iakkhos, Paristhea, The Kharites, Hymenaios, Sabazios.

Notable Stories:

The Marriage to Ariadne

Then I saw Phaedra, Procris, and the lovely
daughter of dangerous Minos, Ariadne.
Theseus tried to bring her back from Crete
to Athens, but could not succeed; the goddess
Artemis killed her on the isle of Dia,
when Dionysus spoke against her.

The Odyssey, Homer, 11. 322-327, translated by Emily Wilson

There are a few stories of how Ariadne and Dionysus came together in marriage. In one, Dionysus traveled around the lands, trying to grow his cult, when he saw the human Ariadne killed or turned into stone during a battle. Dionysus decided to bring her up from the underworld and to Olympus as his immortal wife. Another tale talks about how Ariadne, daughter of the king of Thebes, helped Theseus during the challenge of battling the Minotaur. After, Ariadne and Theseus left on a boat, but Ariadne fell asleep, and Theseus abandoned her. In seeing this, Dionysus decided to take Ariadne as his wife, bringing her back to Olympus. And in yet another story, Ariadne was killed by Artemis, and upon entering the underworld, Dionysus decided to take her as his wife, so he brought her to Olympus.

Discovering Wine

As for Dionysos, Zeus rescued him from the anger of Hera by turning him into a kid; and Hermes gathered him up and took him to some nymphs who lived at Nysa in Asia... After his discovery or the vine, Dionysos was driven mad by Hera and roamed ground Egypt and Syria.

The Library of Greek Mythology, III.4.3, Apollodorus, translated by Robin Hard

When Dionysus was a child, he was taken by Hermes to a group of nymphs and in this journey, the young god discovered the grapevine and how to make wine. Upon turning the grapes into wine, Hera was displeased with this power. So she put a madness on him which caused him to travel all over the lands, but Rhea cured the madness. However, Dionysus continued to introduce grapes and vines to others, creating large groups of followers who participated in revelry and ecstasy.

Hephaestus | Hēphaistos (Ἥφαιστος)

Clear-voiced Muse, sing of Hephaistos,
famous for craft. He and owl-eyed Athena taught
glorious works to earthbound humans,
who used to live like animals in mountain caves.
Now they easily learn skills from Hephaistos,
whose skill is renowned, and live their lives
at ease in their own houses all year around.
Be gracious, Hephaistos: grant excellence and wealth!

Homeric Hymn 20 to Hephaistos, translated by Diane J. Rayor

Described as a bearded man with the tools of a blacksmith, Hephaestus was born of Hera and Zeus, or possibly just Hera or Talos. Earlier descriptions of Hephaestus' birth include Zeus, but later stories speak of Hera as only parent as she wanted to birth a child without a father, and she gave birth to him from her thigh.

What separates Hephaestus from other deities is being described as weak and sickly. He is disfigured or disabled, with a crooked foot that causes lameness. Some translations connect the lameness to a fall perpetuated by Zeus, who was not happy to have a weak son. And in another telling by Homer, Hephaestus had the disfigurement from birth.

In their shame, Hephaestus was thrown out of Olympus by his parents, perhaps after seeing his disfigurement or possibly after throwing him down to cause injury. In some stories, Hephaestus came back with the golden throne and talked his way back into Olympus. In other versions, his brother Ares wanted him to come back, so Ares threatened and came after him, only to be turned away by Hephaestus' weapons. Hephaestus was brought back to Olympus by Dionysus who got him drunk and carried him back in another story.

Hephaestus made the weapons of the gods and was highly revered for metalworking. Often celebrated in places of manufacturing and industry, Hephaestus was seen as being more of the people, though his talents were used in mythical ways. For example, he took Aphrodite as his wife by creating a golden throne for Hera. But when Hera sat down, she was unable to get back up, which Hephaestus used as leverage to convince Hera and Zeus to give Hephaestus Aphrodite's hand in marriage.

Hephaestus was also responsible for creating the magical girdle of Aphrodite, Hermes' winged helmet and sandals, armor for Achilles, the bow and arrows for Eros, and Helios' chariot.

Select Attributes: Fire, Blacksmiths, Volcanoes.

Select Epithets: Klytos (Famous), Klytotekhnês (Famed Worker for Crafts), Polyphrôn (Ingenious), Khalkeus (Bronze or Copper Smith), Amphigyêeis (Crooked Foot).

Select Symbols & Correspondences: Hammer, Tongs, Donkey, Volcanoes, Quail.

Select Partners / Lovers: Charis Aglaea, Aphrodite, Gaia, Kabeiro, Aitna, Atthis/Attis, Athena.

Select Children: The Kabeiroi, Kadmilos, Eukleia, Euthenia, Eupheme, Philphrosyne, The Palikoi, Thaleia, Erikhthonios, Philammon, Pylios.

Notable Stories:

Aphrodite's Affair

> *When Vulcanus [Hephaestus] knew that Venus [Aphrodite] was secretly lying with Mars [Ares], and that he could not oppose his strength, he made a chain of adamant and put it around the bed to catch Mars by cleverness. When Mars came to the rendezvous, the[n] together with Venus fell into the snare so that he could not extricate himself. When Sol reported this to Vulcan, he saw them lying there naked, and summoned all the gods… who saw. As a result, shame frightened Mars so that he did not do this.*
>
> Fabulae from The Myths of Hyginus, Hyginus, 148, translated by Mary Grant

Hephaestus and Aphrodite were married under less than ideal circumstances, as Aphrodite did not want to marry a disfigured blacksmith. They married under the direction of Zeus to ensure no one would fight over the Goddess of Love. As Aphrodite was not willing to stay loyal in a marriage of obligation, she had affairs, most notably with Ares. Hephaestus found out about the affair and made a magical golden net to capture them. This net was so fine and well-crafted that it was impossible to break free from it. Hephaestus brought the two to the gods, still trapped in the net, to Olympus to shame them for their actions. The other gods were not upset at this discovery, though they tried to find a way to punish Ares.

The Creation of Pandora

> *Prometheus, son of Iapetus, first fashioned men from clay. Later Vulcan [Hephaestus], at Jove's [Zeus'] command, made a woman's form from clay. Minerva [Athena] gave it life, and the rest of the gods each gave [s]ome other gift. Because of this they named her Pandora. She was given in marriage to Prometheus' brother Epimetheus. Pyrrha was her daughter, and was said to be the first mortal born.*
>
> Fabulae from The Myths of Hyginus, Hyginus, 142, translated by Mary Grant

In the beginning of creation, everything was bountiful and peaceful. Prometheus was sent into the world to create men out of clay in the image of the gods. He decided to give all men the ability to make fire. But Zeus was not pleased with this and told Hephaestus to make Pandora, the first woman, out of clay and water. She was to be made beautiful and pleasing, to be a gift to the world, but also a burden to mankind. When she was made, Pandora was given a box by Zeus and told to never open it. But she was curious and opened the box, which released the woes of the world. However, upon seeing what she had done, she closed the box quickly, which allowed hope to remain safely in the box, as it was placed there by Prometheus.

Hera | Hērē (Ἥρη)

I sing of gold-enthroned Hera, daughter of Rhea,
statuesque divine queen,
sister and glorious wife of loud-rumbling Zeus.
All the blessed gods in high Olympos
stand in awe and honor her equally
with thunder-loving Zeus.

Homeric Hymn 12 to Hera, translated by Diane J. Rayor

Born of Cronus and Rhea, Hera is the wife of Zeus and queen of the Olympians. By some accounts, Hera was given to daughters of the river to be raised, while others have Hera given to Tethys to be cared for at the request of Rhea. Often depicted with a crown and a scepter, Hera is a leader, but the role is not easy for her. Much of the myth surrounding Hera describes her reactions to Zeus' ongoing infidelities. Described as matronly and regal, Hera is vengeful towards those who offend her.

Sometimes seen in a chariot pulled by peacocks, Hera is a protector of women and attends childbirths, but also is seen to be ashamed of her son, Hephaestus, when it was discovered, he was disfigured at birth. In some stories, Hera cast Hephaestus out of Olympus because he was not what she expected him to be.

Hera was said to be so angry with Paris for choosing Aphrodite as the most beautiful of the gods that Hera aligned herself with the Greeks during the Trojan War. During this war, Zeus did not help Hera, so Hera and Athena went into battle themselves, which angered Zeus enough to send Iris, his messenger, to try to bring them back.

Many myths include Hera's rage at Zeus for not only having affairs, but also having many children outside of their marriage. In addition, she seemed to be so jealous of Zeus having borne

Athena from his forehead, and without her, that Hera gave birth to Hephaestus, Typhaon, and, possibly, Ares without Zeus, just to show she could.

Hera was widely worshiped and revered in ancient cities, often at the same time as Zeus.

Select Attributes: Marriage, Family, Protector of Women.

Select Epithets: Pais (Girl), Nympheuomenê (Betrothed Bride), Khêra (Widow), Gamêlia (of Marriage), Hêniokhê (of the Chariot), Antheia (of the Flowers), Hyperkheiria (Whose Hand is Above).

Select Symbols & Correspondences: Scepter, Cow, Lion, Pomegranate, Peacock, Cuckoo.

Select Partners / Lovers: Zeus.

Select Children: Hebe, Ares, Eileithyia, Hephaestus, Typhaon, The Kharities.

Notable Stories:

Tiresias / Teiresias

> *[Teiresias] caught sight of some snakes coupling near Mount Cyllene, and when he injured the snakes, he was changed from man to a woman; but when he saw the same snakes coupling on a further occasion, he became a man again. And for this reason, when Zeus and Hera were having an argument as to whether men or women gain more pleasure from love-making, they consulted Teiresias. He said that judging the act of love on a scale of ten, men get one part of the pleasure and women nine parts. On that account, Hera turned him blind, but*

Zeus granted him the gift of prophecy; and he lived to be a considerable age.

The Library of Greek Mythology, Apollodorus, III.6.7, translated by Robin Hard

A priest of Zeus, Tiresias, encountered two snakes that were mating. He decided to poke them with a stick, and he was transformed into a woman for seven years. As a woman, Tiresias became a priestess of Hera. But coming upon the snakes again, Tiresias turned back into a man. Zeus and Hera were fascinated by this change and asked Tiresias who experienced more sexual pleasure: a man or a woman. Zeus believed it was women who had more sexual pleasure, and Tiresias agreed. Hearing this, Hera blinded Tiresias, but Zeus gave Tiresias the power of prophecy. Another version says Tiresias was blinded by Hera because he saw her naked. As the curse could not be changed, Athena offered the gift of foresight to Tiresias.

The Seduction of Zeus

Now Hera of the golden throne looked with her eyes upon him
from Olympus, from the pinnacle where she stood…
then she looked toward Zeus sitting on this highest peak of Ida
of the many springs, and hatred grew in her heart….
she set out from her chamber, and summoning Aphrodite
apart from the rest of the gods, she spoke a word to her:
"Could you listen, dear child, to something that I would say,
or would you refuse me, resentful in your heart
because I aid the Danaans, and you the Trojans?"
Then Aphrodite the daughter of Zeus answered her:
"Hera, eldest goddess, daughter of mighty Cronus,
speak what you will: my heart compels me to accomplish it,
if I am able to accomplish it, and if it can be accomplished."
Then with calculated guile lady Hera addressed her:

"Grant me now your power of love and desire, with which you subdue all immortal gods and mortal men.
For I am going to the end of the nourishing earth to visit Ocean, the source of the gods, and mother Tethys,
who in their house nurtured me well and raised me...
I am going to see them, and I will resolve their unending quarrels..."

The Iliad, Homer, Book 14. 253ff, translated by Caroline Alexander

Hera supported the Greeks during the Trojan War, but Zeus had forbidden the gods from going on the battlefield. Knowing they needed more support; Hera planned to put Zeus to sleep to help Poseidon gather more support. To seduce Zeus, Hera traveled to Aphrodite for help. She asked for Aphrodite's magical girdle, as it made a wearer irresistible. With the girdle, Hera seduced Zeus and they made love on Mount Ida. Afterward, Hypnos caused Zeus to fall asleep for enough time to help the Greeks get ahead during the war with the Trojans.

Hermes | Hermēs (Ἑρμης)

I sing to Kyllenian Hermes, Slayer of Argos,
Guardian of Mount Kyllene and Arcadia, rich in flocks,
Luck-bringing messenger of gods, born when Maia,
daughter of Atlas, joined in love with Zeus.
Shunning the crowd of blessed gods, the revered goddess
lived in the shady cave where the son of Kronos
used to lie with her in the dark of night
(while sweet sleep held white-armed Hera)
unnoticed by immortal gods and mortal men.
Son of Zeus and Maia, rejoice in this:
I began with you and will turn to the rest of the hymn.
Hail, Hermes, guide who gives joy and good fortune!

Homeric Hymn 18 to Hermes, translated by Diane J. Rayor

Born of Zeus and Maia or just Zeus or Aphrodite and Dionysus, Hermes is a tricky god. Able to move between worlds, he wears a winged helmet and winged sandals (in later descriptions) to aid his flight. Sometimes described as a youthful man or as an older bearded man, Hermes was a baby when he snuck out of his crib to create the first lyre after stealing Apollo's cattle.

Functioning as a messenger of the gods, Hermes carries a caduceus, a staff with two serpents coiled around it, which could awaken people or put them to sleep. Early writings about Hermes describe him as a psychopomp, helping move people into the underworld upon their death.

Often worshiped in towns to help protect cattle from harm, Hermes would be offered sacrifices for saving flocks from disease. He had knowledge of how to effectively breed animals and how to ensure their protection and safety. As a personal herald to Zeus, Hermes is referenced as holding this special title in numerous writings and described as heaven's herald.

Hermes can bring good luck to people, but also be tricky and deceitful. This juxtaposition made him a valuable god, though he sometimes made decisions that were in his interest rather than for the greater good. For example, Hermes was a part of the creation of Pandora, adding to the box lies, questionable character, and cunning words. It was also purported that Hermes was the one who could share omens with those who favored him, but if you were not in Hermes' favor, you could be cursed with false omens.

Select Attributes: Travel, Flocks, Trade, Protector, Psychopomp, Messenger, Animal Husbandry, Feasts, Sleep, Language, Guide to the Dead, Games, Astronomy, Omens, Dreams, Hospitality, Fertility, Communication.

Select Epithets: Epimêlios (Keeper of the Flocks), Kriophoros (Ram Bearer), Agoraios (of the Marketplace), Dolios (of Crafts), Promakhos (Champion), Herméneutês (Interpreter), Diaktoros (Guide, Messenger), Angelos Athanatôn (Messenger of the Gods), Khrysorrhapis (of the Golden Wand), Mêkhaniôtês (Trickster), Polytropos (Wily), Oiopolos (Sheep Tending), Kharidôtês (Giver of Joy), Eriounês (Luck Bringing), Kydimos (Glorious).

Select Symbols & Correspondences: Caduceus, Ram, Hare, Hawk, Crocus, Rooster, Tortoise, Winged Sandals (Talaria), Goat, Winged Helmet, Phallus.

Select Partners / Lovers: Dryopos, Thymbris, Penelopeia, Kallisto, Aphrodite, Aglauros, Hearse, Kreousa, Daeira.

Select Children: Pan, Hermaphroditus, Eleusis, Priapus, Keryx, Kephalos, Orion.

Notable Stories:

The Seduction of Aphrodite

> *Some, too, have said that Mercury [Hermes] (though others say Anaplades) stirred by Venus's [Aphrodite's] beauty, fell in love with her, and when she permitted no favours, became greatly downcast, as if in disgrace. Jove [Zeus] pitied him, and when Venus was bathing in the river Achelous he sent an eagle to take her sandal to Amythaonia of the Egyptians and give it to Mercury. Venus, in seeking for it, came to him who loved her, and so he, on attaining his desire, as a reward put the eagle in the sky.*
>
> Astronomica Bk 2, from The Myths of Hyginus, Hyginus, 2.16.4, translated and edited by Mary Grant

Like many who encountered Aphrodite, Hermes fell in love with the goddess and wanted her favors. But Aphrodite was not taking suitors, which saddened Hermes immensely. Zeus, upon seeing this sadness, took pity on Hermes and had an eagle steal one of Aphrodite's sandals while she was bathing in the River Achelous. In trying to find what was lost, Aphrodite identified Hermes as the keeper of the missing sandal. There, he was able to tell her of his love. And in doing so, he was so pleased that he placed the eagle in the sky.

Birth of Pan

Tell me, Muse, about Hermes' dear son,
his goat-footed, two-horned, noise-loving son
who roams wooded meadows with dancing nymphs.
The goddesses who scamper up cliffs of sheer rock,
invoking Pan, shepherd god with wild, shining hair,
whose domain includes all snowy crests,
mountain heights, and rocky paths.
He wanders through thick underbrush
now drawn to gentle streams,
now hoofing about steep boulders,
climbing to the highest peak to watch for sheep.

Homeric Hymn 19 to Pan, 1-11, translated by Diane J. Rayor

There are many stories for Pan's birth and his parents, but one story involves Hermes and a tryst with Penelope, the wife of Odysseus. In other stories, Hermes tended the sheep of mortal men and fell in love with Dryopos, a rich man's daughter. She got pregnant and gave birth to Pan, who had goat feet and horns, which upset the midwife. Seeing this reaction, Hermes took the child to Zeus and the other Olympians, who loved the child and called him Pan.

Hestia (Εστια)

Hestia, you tend the sacred hearth
of far-shooting Lord Apollo in holy Pytho,
anointing-oil ever dripping from your braids –
come to this house, come, sharing your heart
with cunning Zeus; bestow grace on my song.

Homeric Hymn 24 to Hestia, translated by Diane J. Rayor

Hestia is the virgin goddess who was calmer and more grounded than her siblings. Her countenance spoke of careful responses to situations rather than reactive measures of her brothers and sisters. It is said this personality enabled her to avoid drama associated with the Olympians. Her critical thinking may also have led to her giving up her seat in the Olympians to Dionysus so she could live a quieter life.

Born of Cronus and Rhea, or possibly of just Cronus or Rhea, Hestia's siblings included Zeus, Demeter, Hades, Hera, and Poseidon. And like her siblings, she was swallowed by Cronus to avoid the prophecy that he would be overthrown by one of his children. Because Zeus was not swallowed, he returned to free his siblings, which allowed Hestia to be another twice-born goddess, as well as the oldest and the youngest, as she was born first, but freed last.

Hestia is a goddess who was most ingrained in ancient Greek culture. As the goddess of the hearth and home, she was in every home in Greece. While she is described as a veiled woman, it is also thought she was more of an idea than a being with human-like qualities. She was the flame families used for cooking and feasting, and she was the flame that needed to be tended so as not to go out. If the flame did go out, it needed to be rekindled in special ways, including by friction or with the focus of the sun's rays.

Hestia presided over sacrifices for all gods, not just sacrifices for her. The hearth was a central gathering place for communities and cities, so her flame was important for civic matters and duties. Because of this, she had many temples and hearths, in addition to being a central figure in homes.

However, Hestia is sometimes reduced to a lesser role with the introduction of Demeter. Much like Gaia's omni-presence in the entirety of the world, Hestia's presence in everyday life made it easier for her to be a part of life versus someone to worship with intricate, discrete rites. When a deity is involved in everything, they become a part of the culture, no less important, though not pedestaled. Unlike other gods, Hestia does not have epithets that are associated with her in Homer's stories, though later sources list titles, which have been included below.

Select Attributes: Hearth, Home, Domestic Life, Family, Community, Sacrifice, Cooking, Feasts, Civic Matters, Sacrifices to the Gods.

Select Epithets:[72] Aidios (Eternal), Basileia (Queen), Chloomorphos (Verdant).

Select Symbols and Correspondences: Flame, Hearth, Kettle, Kettledrum, Chaste-Tree/Flowering Branch, Veil, Robe, Pig.

Select Partners / Lovers: none

Select Children: none

Notable Stories:

Virginity of Hestia

The work of Aphrodite does not please Hestia,

the modest first born of conniving Kronos
(last born, too, through the plan of Zeus).
Wooed by Poseidon and Apollo, she was unwilling
and hard, refusing their offers of marriage.
Touching the head of Zeus who bears the aegis,
she swore a great oath, since then fulfilled,
to remain forever virgin, divine among goddesses.
Instead of marriage, Father Zeus gave her a prize:
Hestia rests at the hearth, the highest honor.
All people revere her in every temple,
Hestia, the most august of the gods.

Homeric Hymn 5 to Aphrodite, 21-32, translated by Diane J. Rayor

Like other virgin goddesses, Hestia went to Zeus to have him promise she would always be a virgin and she would not be promised to anyone in marriage. It is said she made this request to Zeus after Poseidon and Apollo both tried to woo her.

Priapus

Shall I pass over or relate thy disgrace, rubicund Priapus? It is a short story, but a very merry one. Cybele, whose brow is crowned with a coronet of towers, invited the eternal gods to her feast. She invited also the satyrs and those rural divinities, the nymphs... It is unlawful, and it would be tedious, to narrate the banquet of the gods... Vesta [Hestia] lay and careless took her peaceful rest, just as she was, her head low laid and propped upon a sod. But the ruddy guardian of gardens courted nymphs and goddesses, and to and fro he turned his roving steps. He spied Vesta too; it is doubtful whether he took her for a nymph or knew her to be Vesta; he himself said that he knew her not... It chanced that Silenus had left the ass, on which he rode, on the banks of a babbling brook. The god of the long Hellespont was going to begin, when the ass uttered an ill-timed bray. Frightened by the deep voice, the goddess started up.

Fasti, Ovid, VI 319 ff, translated by Sir James George Frazer

Hestia slept in a field when Priapus, a vegetation god, found her and tried to rape her. He was unsuccessful as a donkey saw him arrive and made a loud noise that alerted Hestia of his presence. Priapus was punished by the other gods and sent away for his actions.

Poseidon | Poseidōn (Ποσειδων)

I begin to sing of the great god Poseidon
who shifts the earth and barren sea,
god of the waters, and of Helike and wide Aigai.
Earthshaker, the gods allotted you a double honor
as tamer of horses and savior of ships.
Farewell, Poseidon, blue-haired god who holds earth;
with a kind heart, Blessed One, aid those who sail.

Homeric Hymn 22 to Poseidon, translated by Diane J. Rayor

God of the sea, born of Rhea and Cronus, Poseidon is sibling to Demeter, Hades, Hera, and Hestia, and rescued by Zeus from being trapped inside of his father, Cronus. In some versions of Poseidon's birth, he is hidden away by Rhea so Cronus can't swallow him. Instead, Rhea gave Cronus a horse to eat while Poseidon was hidden in a flock of lambs.

Another twice-born Olympian, Poseidon was one of the three gods assigned to different realms after the War of the Titans. Zeus was granted Olympus and Hades ruled the Underworld. While this means Poseidon has a lot of power, he is not as powerful as his brothers. The bottom of the Aegean Sea is home to the palace of Poseidon, and where he can travel to in a chariot. He created horses and taught man about handling horses. Sometimes, Poseidon is shown riding a horse or to have a chariot that is led by two or four horses.

Poseidon has ultimate power over the winds and the waters. He conjures the weather to hinder certain actions from happening, while also clearing away obstacles. To do this, he used his trident, a three-pointed spear, directing it at the waters, winds, or rocks.

With lovers from all genders, Poseidon fathered children and other beings with his wife, Amphitrite, as well as with gods and mortals. Many stories describe Poseidon as having raped multiple beings, including Demeter and Medusa. There are also stories of Asteria and Corone who Poseidon attempted to rape, but Asteria turned herself into a quail and Athena turned Corone into a crow to keep them from his advances.

Select Attributes: Sea, Earthquakes, Horses, Floods.

Select Epithets: Basileus (King), Pelagaios (of the Sea), Asphalios (Secures Safe Voyage), Ennosigaios (Shaker of the Sea), Hippios (of the Horses), Phytalmios (Plant Nurturer), Genethlios (of the Kin), Laoitês (of the People).

Select Symbols and Correspondences: Trident, Water, Sea, Ocean, Boulder, Sea Creatures, Bull, Horse, Dolphin, Pine Tree, Wild Celery, Half-Horse/Half-Fish.

Select Partners / Lovers: Amphitrite, Cleito, Melia, Nerites, Pelops, Patroclus, Tyro, Demeter, Medusa, Caenis/Caeneus.

Select Children: Triton, Rhode, Benthesicyme, Theseus, Arion, Despoina, Polyphemus, Orion, Belus, Agenor, Pelias, Neleus, Atlas, Pegasus, Chrysaor, Kymopoleia, Bellerophon, Cyclops.

Notable Stories:

The Rape of Caenis/Caeneus

Elatus's daughter, Caenis, loveliest of the virgins of Thessaly, was famous for her beauty, a girl longed for in vain, the object of many suitors throughout the neighbouring cities and your own (since she was one of your people, Achilles). Perhaps Peleus also would have tried to wed her, but he had already taken your mother in marriage, or she was promised to your father. Caenis would not agree to any marriage, but (so rumour has it) she was walking along a lonely beach, and the god took her by force. When Neptune had enjoyed his new love he said: "Make your wish, without fear of refusal. Ask for what you most want!" (The same rumour mentioned this.)

"This injury evokes the great desire never to be able to suffer any such again. Grant I might not be a woman: you will have given me everything," Caenis said. She spoke the last words in a deeper tone that might have been the sound of a man's voice. So it was: the god of the deep ocean had already accepted her wish, and had granted, over and above it, that as a man Caeneus would be protected from all wounds, and never fall to the sword. Caeneus, the Atracides, left, happy with his gifts, and spent his time in manly pastimes, roaming the Thessalian fields.'

Metamorphoses, Ovid, XII 195 ff, translated by A.S. Kline

While Caenis walked along the sea, Poseidon saw her and decided he had to have her. He raped her but offered a wish in return. Traumatized, Caenis asked to be turned into a man so she would never have to experience a rape again, which Poseidon granted.

Laying with Demeter

> *When Demeter was wandering in search of her daughter, she was followed, it is said, by Poseidon, who lusted after her. So she turned, the story runs, into a mare, and grazed with the mares of Oncius; realizing that he was outwitted, Poseidon too changed into a stallion and enjoyed Demeter.*
>
> Description of Greece, Pausanias, 8.25.5, translated by W.H.S. Jones

Poseidon was entranced by the goddess Demeter, who realized that he wanted to rape her. To outwit him, Demeter turned into a horse, but Poseidon realized this and became a stallion and they laid together. This encounter resulted in the birth of Arion, a horse that speaks in human languages.

Zeus (Ζευς)

> *I will sing of Zeus, the best and greatest of gods,*
> *far-seeing king, the accomplisher, who keeps Themis*
> *deep in discussion as she sits leaning toward him.*
> *Be gracious, far-seeing Kronion, greatest and most glorious!*
>
> Homeric Hymn 23 to Zeus, translated by Diane J. Rayor

Born of Rhea and Cronus, Zeus presided over Olympus as the leader, king, or father of all the gods. He rescued his swallowed siblings by getting a potion from Metis to have Cronus regurgitate them or birthing them from his forehead. All deities are under his rule, which extended to mortals and beings, with him distributing favor and punishment. Armed with thunderbolt and lightning, Zeus destroyed those who he saw fit to kill.

Raised by Gaia to be spared by Cronus, Zeus went to live in Crete to avoid harm. To make sure Cronus didn't realize this, Rhea wrapped up a stone in a blanket and gave it to Cronus to eat. Upon disgorging the children, Zeus took the stone and put it at Delphi as an example to man. And the Cyclops gave Zeus the thunderbolt in exchange for being freed alongside the others, as prophesied by Gaia.

Pictured with a white beard and a lightning bolt in hand, Zeus' power was challenged at every turn once he was the king of Olympus. When Gaia found out Zeus imprisoned her children, the Titans, and banished them to Tartarus, she sent Giants to overtake him. This battle is not detailed in all texts, but Apollodorus described the Gigantomachy[73] as a time when a prophecy said the Titans could not be defeated by just the gods, that a mortal must also help (Herakles), and a special herb would also prevent their demise. Zeus told Helios, Selene, and Eos to stop the heavens from shining so Zeus could harvest the herb, pharmakon. When the strongest giant fell in love with Hera, Zeus stopped him with a lightning bolt and Herakles killed the giant with an arrow.

Often seen as a leader and a victor, Zeus was married to Hera and had multiple affairs outside of his marriage, which angered her. Zeus' affairs had consequences across the gods and the relationships of the gods, while also resulting in children who would go on to greatness.

Select Attributes: Sky, Weather, Fate, King.

Select Epithets: Ombrios (of the Rain), Skotitas (Dark), Keraunios (of the Thunderbolt), Astrapaios (of the Lightning), Labrandeus (Furious), Konios (of the Dust), Basileus (King, Ruler), Hypatos (Most High), Koryphaios (Leader), Ktêsios (of the House), Moiragetês (Leader of the Fates), Sêmaleos (Giver of Signs), Mêkhaneus (Contriver), Plousios (of Wealth),

Palamnaios (Punisher of Murderers), Katharsios (of Ritual Purification), Meilikhios (Merciful), Stratios/Areios (of War).

Select Symbols & Correspondences: Thunderbolt, Eagle, Oak, Bull, Olive Tree, Throne.

Select Partners / Lovers: Hera, Metis, Aphrodite, Asteria, Demeter, Dione, Eurynome, Gaia, Hybris, Calliope, Leto, Mnemosyne, Nemesis, Persephone, Selene, Selene, Styx, Themis, Thetis.

Select Children: Ares, Hephaestus, Athena, Aphrodite, Apollo, Artemis, Hermes, Persephone, Dionysus, Perseus, Herakles, Helen, Minos, Muses, Moraie, Horai, Nymphai, Kharities, Hebe, Eris, Pan, Harmonia, and more.

Notable Stories:

War of the Titans

> *But the son of Kronos, and the other immortal gods whom lovely-haired Rhea bore in intimacy with Kronos, brought them up again into the light, on Earth's advice. For she told them everything at length – that with their help they would win victory and their proud claim. For long they had fought against each other in fierce combat, and the struggle gave them pain at heart, the Titan gods and those that were born of Kronos: the proud Titans from high Othrys, and from Olympus the gods, givers of blessings, whome lovely-haired Rhea bore bedded with Kronos. They had been fighting each other continually now for ten full years, and the fight gave them pain at heart; and to neither side came the solution or end of the bitter strife, and the outcome of the war was equally balanced. But when Zeus provided those allies with full sustenance, nectar and ambrosia,*

such as the gods themselves eat, and the proud spirit waxed in all their breasts, then the father of gods and men spoke to them.

Theogony, Hesiod, pp 21-22, translated by M. L. West

Titanomachy was a 10-year war between the new gods and the Titans, which started when Cronus overtook his father, Uranus, by severing his genitals, at the request of Gaia. This action also bore Aphrodite, freed the monsters and Cyclops, and cast Uranus to Tartarus, an abyss of torture used punish wrongdoers. Cronus was still afraid of the prophecy his father faced and swallowed his children as well as the Cyclops and the monsters again. Zeus was spared this fate of swallowing and came back to free those imprisoned. In doing so, Zeus waged war against his father and the Titans. The Olympians won the war, and the Titans were imprisoned in Tartarus, guarded by the monsters. In some accounts, Zeus freed the Titans once his power was solidified.

Zeus and Typhon/Typhoeus

Now when Zeus had driven the Titans out of heaven, the huge Earth bore as her youngest child, Typhoeus, being united in intimacy with Tartarus by golden Aphrodite. His arms were employed with feats of strength, and the legs of the powerful god are tireless. Out of his shoulders came a hundred fearsome snake-heads with black tongues flickering, and the eyes in his strange heads flashed fire under the brows; and there were voices in all his fearsome heads, giving out every kind of indescribable sound..... When Zeus had accumulated his strength, then, and taken his weapons, the thunder, lightning, and smoking bolt, he lept from Olympus and struck, and he scorched all the strange heads of the dreadful monster on every side.

Theogony, Hesiod, pp 27-28, translated by M. L. West

Once Zeus' position in Olympus was secure, Typhon challenged him. Typhon was a sea monster, snake-like, who wanted power over all the worlds. While the battle was dramatic, Zeus easily defeated Typhon with thunder, lightning, and a bolt and banished Typhon to Tartarus. Other versions of the story have Typhon finding his way into Zeus' palace before Zeus defeated him.

Minor Olympians

While the Olympians are listed as the main gods in Greek mythology, there are other deities who were a part of Olympus. They had specific duties and helped attend to the gods.

Some of minor gods and demi-gods include:

- **Asclepius** – Physician who could restore the dead to life; Zeus destroyed him with a thunderbolt because of this unnatural talent, but he was later elevated to godhood.
- **Eileithyia** – Goddess of childbirth and midwifery; daughter of Hera and Zeus.
- **Eros** – God of love and sex; son of Aphrodite and Ares or parentless.
- **Erotes** – Winged gods of love; children of Aphrodite or Zephyrus and Iris.
- **Harmonia** – Goddess of peace and harmony; daughter of Aphrodite and Ares or daughter of Zeus and Electra.
- **Hebe** – Goddess of youth; daughter of Hera and Zeus; lover of Herakles.
- **Horae / Horai (Hôra / Hôrai)** – Goddesses of the seasons, peace, justice, and good order: Eirene, Eunomia, and Dike; daughters of Zeus and Themis; guided the constellations and the Sun.

- **Hygeia** – Goddess of health, hygiene, and cleanliness; daughter of Asclepius and Epione.
- **Hymenaeus** – God of marriage and marriage-song; son of Apollo and a Muse (Terpsichore, Urania, or Calliope).
- **Iris** – Goddess of the rainbow and divine messenger of the Olympians, daughter of Thaumas and Electra and sister of the Harpies; servant of Hera and Zeus.
- **Graces / Kharites / Charities** – Three or more goddesses of charm, beauty, joy, creativity, nature, and more; possibly daughters of Zeus and Eurynome.
- **Moirae / Moirai (The Fates)** – Three sisters of fate and destiny: Clotho (spinner), Lachesis (allotter), and Atropos (inevitable); daughters of Themis and Zeus.
- **Muses** – Goddesses of music, song, poetry, literature, and the arts; daughters of Zeus and Mnemosyne; Calliope/ Kalliope, Clio, Polyhymnia, Euterpe, Terpsichore, Erato, Melpomene, Thalia, and Urania.
- **Nike** – Goddess of victory; daughter of Styx and Pallas.
- **Paeon** – Physician of the Olympian gods; no known parents.
- **Pothos** – God of sexual longing; son of Aphrodite or Zephyrus and Iris.
- **Tyche** – Goddess of fortune and luck; daughter of Oceanus and Tethys.

Chthonian Gods – Gods & Beings of the Underworld

Known as Theoi Khthonioi, the underworld gods are ruled by Persephone and Hades. Located in Hades (named for the ruler), these gods meet travelers after their death to bring them to their afterlife.

It seems wise to introduce Hades and Persephone as they do not show up as Olympian gods, as their realm was so far away from Olympus, but played important roles.

Hades | Haidês (Ἀιδης)

You dwell below the earth,
O strong-spirited one,
a meadow in Tartaros,
thick-shaded and dark.
Sceptered Chthonic Zeus,
please accept this sacrifice,
O Plouton, holder of the keys
to the whole earth.
To mankind you give
the wealth of the year's fruits,
yours is the third portion,
earth, queen of all,
seat of the gods,
mighty lap of mortals.
Your throne rests
on a dark realm,
the realm of distant, of untiring,
of windless, and of impassive Hades;
it does rest on gloomy Acheron,
the river who girds the roots of the earth.
All-receiver, master of death,
master of mortals, host of many,
Euboulos, you once took as your bride
pure Demeter's daughter:
you tore her away from the meadow,
and through the sea
you carried her to an Attic cave
upon your steeds—
it was the district of Eleusis,
where the gates to Hades are.
You alone were born to judge
deeds obscure and conspicuous.

Holiest and illustrious ruler of all,
frenzied god,
you delight in the respect
and in the reverence of your worshippers.
I summon you, come with favor,
come with joy to the initiates.

Orphic Hymn 18 to Pluton, translated by Apostolos N. Athanassakis and Benjamin M. Wolkow

King of the Underworld, ruler of the dead, Hades is the child of Cronus and Rhea, another child devoured by Cronus and freed by Zeus. After the War of the Titans, Hades was one of three who were given a realm to rule after drawing lots, and he was granted the underworld. Because of this, Hades is associated with death rites and ensuring the dead are buried appropriately. This underworld god is connected to the idea of wealth in the earth, or the hidden treasures of the fertile soil and metals, like silver and gold.

He has a long, dark beard, and sometimes sits on a black throne. But the Greeks were afraid of Hades, so he does not show up in art or writings as much as other gods.

Much of the attention Hades gets is in relation to the way Persephone becomes his wife. The most common story is that he takes her down to the underworld, with some tales including him raping her. Other stories talk about how Zeus and/or Gaia help to get Persephone to Hades. In some accounts, Hades asked Zeus for help in finding him a wife. Other writings talk about how Gaia helped Hades by making sure certain flowers would entice the young maiden.

Select Attributes: Death, Underworld, Burial, Hidden Wealth.

Select Epithets: Ploutôn (of Wealth), Polydegmôn (Host of Many), Nekrodegmôn (Receiver of the Dead).

Select Symbols & Correspondences: Cornucopia, Scepter, Screech Owl, Narcissus, Cypress, Asphodel, White Poplar, Mint, Cerberus, Serpent, Keys, Pomegranate, Chariot, Cattle.

Select Partners / Lovers: Persephone, Leuce, Minthe, Demeter.

Select Children: Macaria, Zagreus, Dionysus, Erinyes.

Notable Stories:

Cerberus (Cerberos) & Herakles (Heracles)

> *As a twelfth labour, he [Herakles] was ordered to fetch Cerberos from Hades. Cerberus had three dog heads, the tail of a dragon, and on his back, the heads of all kinds of snakes... He made his way to Tainaron in Laconia, where the mouth of the descent to Hades is located, and descended through it. When the souls caught sight of him, they fled, except for Meleager and the Gorgon Medusa... Wanting to procure blood for the souls, he slaughtered one of the cattle of Hades; but their herdsman, Menoites, son of Ceuthonymos, challenged him to a wrestling match. Heracles seized him round the middle and broke his ribs, but let him go when Persephone interceded. When he asked Pluto for Cerberos, Pluto told him to take the beast if he could overpower it without using any of the weapons that he was carrying. Discovering Cerberos by the gates of Acheron, Heracles, sheathed in his breastplate and fully covered by his lion's skin, grasped its head between his arms and never relaxed his grip and stranglehold on the beast until he had broken its will.*
>
> The Library of Greek Mythology, Apollodorus, II.5.12, translated by Robin Hard

Herakles traveled to the underworld and gave the souls blood by slaughtering Hades' cattle. The keeper of the cattle was not pleased, and tried to wrestle him, but Herakles was too strong. After Persephone stopped the fight, Herakles asked Hades for Cerberus, which was granted under certain conditions, which Herakles met. As the last of his twelve labors, Herakles showed Cerberus to Eurystheus, and then returned the creature to Hades.

A Favor for Orpheus

> *When his [Orpheus'] wife Eurydice died from a snake-bite, he went down to Hades in the hope of bringing her up, and persuaded Pluto [Hades] to send her back to earth. Pluto promised to do so, provided that on the way up Orpheus never looked round until he had arrived back at his house. But Orpheus failed to obey him, and turning round, he caught sight of his wife, and she had to return below.*
>
> The Library of Greek Mythology, Apollodorus, I.3.2, translated by Robin Hard

When Orpheus' wife, Eurydice, died from a snake bite, Orpheus traveled to the underworld to get her back from Hades. Hades was entranced by music Orpheus played and promised Orpheus he could have his wife back if he would not look back at her as they traveled out of the underworld to their home. But Orpheus looked back, and Eurydice died again, and Orpheus was not allowed to return to the underworld again.

Persephone | Persephonê (Περσεφονη)

> *Persephone, blessed daughter*
> *of great Zeus, sole offspring*
> *of Demeter, come and accept*

this gracious sacrifice.
Much-honored spouse of Plouton,
discreet and life-giving,
you command the gates of Hades
in the bowels of the earth,
lovely-tressed Praxidike,
pure bloom of Deo,
mother of the Erinyes,
queen of the nether world,
secretly sired by Zeus
in clandestine union.
Mother of loud-roaring,
many-shaped Eubouleus,
radiant and luminous,
playmate of the Seasons,
revered and almighty,
maiden rich in fruits,
brilliant and horned,
only-beloved of mortals,
in spring you take your joy
in the meadow of breezes,
you show your holy figure
in branches teeming with grass-green fruits,
in autumn you were made
a kidnapper's bride.
You alone are life and death
to toiling mortals,
O Persephone, you nourish all,
always, and kill them, too.
Hearken, O blessed goddess,
send forth the fruits of the earth
as you blossom in peace,
and in gentle-handed health
bring a blessed life

and a splendid old age to him who is sailing
to your realm, O queen,
and to mighty Plouton's kingdom.

Orphic Hymn 29 to Persephone, translated by Apostolos N. Athanassakis and Benjamin M. Wolkow

Born of Zeus and Demeter or Zeus and Nyx, Persephone became the Queen of the Underworld when Hades took her or when she traveled to the Underworld for the role. Zeus helped Hades get Persephone and Gaia created the flowers to attract young Kore (maiden Persephone) to separate her from other goddesses in the field. Most stories focus on Persephone being taken to the underworld and made to stay there as she ate pomegranate seeds and when you ate food of the land of dead, you could not return to the land of the living.

Worshipped alongside her mother, Demeter, Persephone is a goddess of the spring too, as she returns every six months, which allows for Demeter's grief to subside and things to grow again. Persephone is celebrated as part of the Eleusinian Mysteries, a ritual that allowed participants to follow mother and daughter, while remembering the passage of life and dead.

Select Attributes: Spring, Underworld, Necromancy, Growth, Curses, Ghosts.

Select Epithets: Kore/Korê, Kourê (Maiden), Khthonia (of the Earth), Karpophoros (Bringer of Fruit), Sôteira (Savior), Megala Thea (Great Goddess), Hagnê (Holy One), Daeira (Knowing One), Praxidikê (Exacter of Justice).

Select Symbols & Correspondences: Asphodel, Pomegranates, Pomegranate Seeds, Grain, Wheat, Torch.

Select Partners / Lovers: Hades, Zeus, Adonis.

Select Children: Zagreus, Melinoe, The Erinyes.

Notable Stories:

Kore & the Underworld

When Zeus ordered Pluto [Hades] to send Kore [Persephone] back to earth, Pluto, to prevent her from remaining too long with her mother, gave her a pomegranate seed to eat, and failing to foresee what the consequence would be, she ate it. When Ascalaphos, son of Acheron and Gorgyra, bore witness against her, Demeter placed a heavy rock over him in Hades, but Persephone was forced to stay with Pluto for a third of every year, and the rest she spent with the gods.

The Library of Greek Mythology, Apollodorus, I.5.3, translated by Robin Hard

Hades found out that Persephone was going to be taken back by Zeus, and to make sure this didn't happen, Hades gave Persephone some pomegranate seeds to eat. In doing so, she would need to remain in the underworld for part of the year, ensuring she would still be married to Hades and remain his consort.

Peirithoos / Pirithous

Theseus came to an agreement with Peirithoos that both would marry daughters of Zeus. With the aid of Peirithoos, he abducted Helen (then aged twelve) from Sparta for himself, and then, in the hope of winning Persephone as a bride for Peirithoos, made his way down to Hades….. When Theseus

arrived in Hades with Peirithoos, he became the victim of a trick. For on the pretence that they were about to enjoy his hospitality as guests, Hades asked them to sit down first on the Chair of Forgetfulness; and they became stuck to it and were held down by coils of snakes. Peirithoos remained a prisoner in Hades ever after.

The Library of Greek Mythology, Apollodorus, Epit. 1: 23-24, translated by Robin Hard

Persephone was meant to be stolen to become the wife of Peirithoos, but Hades realized what was happening and trapped him in a chair that made him forget what he wanted, imprisoning him forever in the underworld.

Other gods and beings of the underworld include:

- **Aeacus** – Underworld judge who was once a king of Aegina; rewarded by the gods with this role.
- **Acheron** – God of the underworld River of Pain; guarded the borders.
- **Amphiaraus** – Prophet daemon,[74] once a seer and war hero; swallowed by the earth during battle.
- **Arae** – Female spirits of curses, especially on murderers.
- **Ascalaphus** – Son of Acheron, possibly a daemon, that tended Hades' orchards; turned into an owl by Demeter for reporting that Persephone ate the pomegranate seed.
- **Cacodaemones** – Underworld spirits sent to inflict harm.
- **Cerberus** – Three-headed hound of Hades who guarded the underworld's entrance.
- **Ceuthonymus** – Daemon whose name means 'named-in-the-depths' or 'hidden-name'.
- **Charon** – Daemon who brought the souls of the dead in a boat across Acheron's streams into Hades.

- **Cocytus** – God of the underworld River of Tears and Wailing.
- **Cronus / Kronos** – *See Titans.*
- **Daerira** – Nymph[75] and companion of Persephone.
- **Empusa** – Underworld daemon with flaming hair, the leg of a goat, and a leg of bronze.
- **Epiales** – Daemon of nightmares.
- **Erebus** – Primeval god of darkness with mists that filled Hades and the hollows of the earth.
- **Erinyes (Furies)** – Goddesses of vengeance and retribution.
- **Eurynomus** – Daemon with blue-black skin and a bird-like head who stripped the flesh from corpses.
- **Gorgyra** – Nymph and wife of Acheron.
- **Hecate / Hekate** – *See They Might (also) be Titans.*
- **Hermes Chthonius** – Guide for the dead who led the ghosts to their final resting place.
- **Hypnos / Hypnus** – God of sleep who lived in a silent realm on the borders of Hades.
- **Keres** – Daemones of violent death and disease who took the souls from the dying on battlefields.
- **Lamia** – Daemones who appeared as beautiful women to seduce and kill young men.
- **Lampades** – Torch-bearing underworld nymphs who served Hecate; guides for initiates of the Eleusinian Mysteries to their final resting place in Elysium.
- **Lethe** – Goddess of the underworld River of Oblivion; helped dead forget their former lives after a sip of the river water.
- **Leuce** – Nymph abducted by Hades to the Eleusinian fields and turned into a white poplar.
- **Macaria** – Goddess of blessed death who led the initiates of the Eleusinian Mysteries.

- **Melinoe** – Daemon with one white side and one black side who led ghosts to haunt the earth.
- **Menoetes / Menoites** – Daemon who herded Hades' black-skinned cattle.
- **Minos** – Judge of the dead, once a king of Crete; rewarded with this role for establishing laws on earth.
- **Minthe** – Nymph turned to dust and then a mint plant by Persephone when the Queen of the Underworld realized Hades loved Minthe; the mint plant was gifted to Hades.
- **Moirae / Moirai / Fates** – *See Minor Olympians.*
- **Mormolyceia** – Daemones like the Lamiae.
- **Oneiri** – Daemones sent to bring false dreams or truthful dreams.
- **Orphne** – Nymph and wife of Acheron.
- **Pyriphlegethon** – God of the River of Fire.
- **Rhadamanthys** – Judge of the Dead and king of the Elysian Fields; rewarded for being a just lawmaker on earth.
- **Styx** – *See Primordial Gods.*
- **Tartarus** – *See Primordial Gods.*
- **Thanatus / Thanatos** – Winged daemon of death.

Theoi Halioi / Einalioi – Gods & Beings of the Sea

The sea gods and other beings were under the rule of Poseidon and the queen, Amphitrite.

- **Aegaeon** (the name men use) / **Briareus** (the name gods use) – God of storms; one of the 100-handed Hecatoncheires.
- **Aegaeus** – God of violent storms.
- **Aeolus** – King of the winds that held back winds until the gods directed their release.
- **Acheilus** – Daemon in the form of a shark.

- **Amphitrite** – Goddess queen of the sea and Poseidon's wife who created fish, dolphins, seals, and whales.
- **Aphros** – Fish-tailed centaur and god of sea foam; helped carry Aphrodite to shore during her birth.
- **Aphrodite** – *See Olympians.*
- **Argyra** – Nymph whose name means 'silvery one'.
- **Benthesicyme** – Nymph and daughter of Poseidon, whose name means 'deep wave'.
- **Bythos** – Fish-tailed sea-centaur, whose name means 'sea depths'; helped Aphrodite to shore during her seafoam birth.
- **Cabeiro** – Nymph and goddess of the Samothracian Mysteries who had a child with Hephaestus.
- **Calliste** – Nymph of the island of Calliste.
- **Capheira** – Nymph nurse of Poseidon.
- **Carcinus** – Gigantic crab who fought the Hydra in a battle against Herakles; placed among the stars as the constellation Cancer.
- **Cetea** – Monsters sent on missions by Poseidon; killed in their efforts.
- **Ceto** – Ancient goddess, whose name means 'whale' or 'sea monster,' ruled monsters and the sea depths.
- **Charybdis** – Daemon of whirlpools chained to the sea bed and caused the tides with breathing.
- **Cymopoleia** – Nymph of high storm waves.
- **Delphin** – Leader of dolphins who became a constellation for helping Poseidon win Amphitrite.
- **Doris** – Mother of the 50 Nereides with husband, Nereus, who watched the interaction of freshwater and brine.
- **Eidothea** – Prophetic nymph.
- **Echidna** – Dragon who was half serpent and half nymph; born of sea scum or Ceto and Phorcys.

- **Electra / Elektra** – Wife of Thaumas and mother of Iris and the Harpies; nymph of the amber-colored clouds that occur during rainbows as the sunlight returns.
- **Erotes** – *See Minor Olympians.*
- **Eurybia** – Ancient goddess who shifted the power of the sea.
- **Galatea** – One of the 50 Nereids associated with the milky white swirling of brine in water.
- **Galene** – One of the 50 Nereids and goddess of calm seas.
- **Glaucus** – Human who turned into a fish-tailed immortal after eating a magical herb; unclear parentage.
- **Gorgons** – Three daemones and daughters of Ceo and Phorcys, depicted with snakes for hair, bronze claws, wings, and tusks.
- **Graeae** – Three gray-haired daemones, who shared one tooth and one eye.
- **Halia** – Nymph of the brine; raped by her sons and leapt into the water in shame.
- **Haliae** – Nymph daughters of Poseidon.
- **Harpies / Harpyie** – Winged sea daemones, daughters of Thaumas and Electra; half-human, half-birds who presided over whirlwinds, water spouts, and violent storm gusts.
- **Helle** – Goddess nymph rescued by Poseidon and turned into a sea goddess.
- **Hippocamps** – Fish-tailed horses who drew the chariot of Poseidon.
- **Ichthyes** – Divine fish who brought Aphrodite ashore during her birth; rewarded by turning into the constellation Pisces.
- **Ladon** – Monstrous, hundred-headed serpent and guard of the western sea.
- **Lamia** – *See Chthonian Gods – Gods & Beings of the Underworld.*

- **Leimenides** – Nymphs of freshwater lakes.
- **Leucothea** – Goddess and protector of sailors and fishermen.
- **Naiads** – Nymphs of the sources of freshwater: springs, fountains, streams, rivers, and lakes.
- **Nereids** – 50 goddess nymphs who provided fish and protected sailors.
- **Nephelae** – Nymphs of the clouds.
- **Nereids** – *See Theoi Halioi / Einalioi – Gods & Beings of the Sea.*
- **Nereus** – Ancient fish-tailed god with 50 Nereid daughters who watched over fish and sea salt.
- **Nerites** – Daemon transformed into shellfish by Aphrodite.
- **Oceanids** – Nymphs of earth's freshwater and heaven's moist breezes and rain clouds; daughters of Oceanus.
- **Oceanus** – *See Titans.*
- **Oeolyca** – Nymph daughter of Briareus and Cymopoleia whose name meant 'lone wolf'; presided over waves of floods and storm surges.
- **Palaemon** – Protector god of sailors and fishermen; a boy who was turned into a god after leaping into the sea to avoid the wrath of his father who was driven mad by Hera.
- **Pallas** – *See They Might (also) be Titans.*
- **Phorcys** – Ancient god of the dangers of the sea.
- **Pontus** – *See Primordial Gods.*
- **Poseidon** – *See Olympians.*
- **Proseoous Daemones** – Evil daemones and children of Poseidon who haunted the dark caverns.
- **Proteus** – Shapeshifting, prophetic god who herded Poseidon's seals.
- **Psamathe** – One of 50 Nereids and goddess of sandy beaches.

- **Rhode** – Nymph daughter of Poseidon and goddess of the island of the same name.
- **Sirens** – Three daemones with the heads of women and the bodies of birds who lured men to their deaths.
- **Scylla** – Monstrous daemon with the upper body of a nymph, the tail of a fish, and a ring of six dog-heads around her waist.
- **Telchines** – Daemones who conjured storms and droughts.
- **Tethys** – *See Titans.*
- **Thalassa** – *See Primordial Gods.*
- **Thaumas** – Ancient god of the wonders of the sea; father of Iris and the Harpies.
- **Thetis** – *See Primordial Gods.*
- **Thoosa** – Nymph and mother of the Polyphemus by Poseidon; linked to fast currents and riptides.
- **Triteia** – Nymph and companion of Ares.
- **Triton** – Poseidon's herald who blew a conch shell horn to calm the waves.
- **Tritones** – Fish-tailed daemones of the sea; male counterparts of the sea nymphs.

Theoi Ouranioi / Meteoroi – Gods & Beings of Sky & Weather

The gods and beings of the sky and the weather were presided over by Zeus and Hera in Olympus.

- **Aeolus** – *See Theoi Halioi / Einalioi – Gods & Beings of the Sea.*
- **Aether** – *See Primordial Gods.*
- **Anemi** – Gods of the four directional winds and heralds of the four seasons, including Boreas, Zephyros, Euros, and Notos.

- **Anemoi** – Daemones of violent storm winds released at the gods' request.
- **Arce** – *See They Might (also) be Titans.*
- **Astraeus** – *See They Might (also) be Titans.*
- **Astra Planeti** – Gods of the five wandering-stars or planets.
- **Astrothesiae** – Spirits or living forms of the heavenly constellations.
- **Atlas** – *See They Might (also) be Titans.*
- **Aura** – *See They Might (also) be Titans.*
- **Aurae** – Nymphs of the breezes.
- **Boreas** – God of the North Wind whose breath signaled the winter and the coming cold.
- **Chaos** – *See Primordial Gods.*
- **Chione** – Goddess of snow and daughter of Boreas.
- **Chronos** – *See Primordial Gods.*
- **Cyclopes** – *See They Might (also) be Titans.*
- **Eos** – *See They Might (also) be Titans.*
- **Eosphorus** – God of the morning or dawn star, Venus.
- **Eurus** – God of the East Wind who brought forth the autumn season.
- **Harpies / Harpyie** – *See Theoi Halioi / Einalioi – Gods & Beings of the Sea.*
- **Hecatoncheires** – *See They Might (also) be Titans.*
- **Helios** – *See They Might (also) be Titans.*
- **Hemera** – *See Primordial Gods.*
- **Hera** – *See Olympians.*
- **Hearse** – Goddess of morning dew.
- **Hesperides** – Three goddesses of sunsets who tended a tree of golden apples given to Zeus and Hera at their wedding by Gaia.
- **Hesperus** – God of the evening star, Venus.
- **Horae / Horai** – *See Minor Olympians.*

- **Hyades** – Nymphs of the five stars of the constellation Hyades; daughters of Atlas; heralded the beginning of spring rainy month.
- **Iris** – *See Minor Olympians.*
- **Menae** – Nymphs of the 50 new moons of the Olympiad and daughters of Selene.
- **Nephelae** – Nymphs of the clouds and daughters of Oceanus.
- **Notus** – God of the wet and stormy South Wind who heralded the month of summer.
- **Oceanides** – Daughters of Oceanus, including Nephelae and Aurae.
- **Oreithyia** – Goddess of cold, gusty mountain winds and wife of Boreas.
- **Pleiades** – Nymphs of the stars of the constellation Pleiades and daughters of Atlas.
- **Selene** – *See They Might (also) be Titans.*
- **Uranus / Ouranos** – *See Primordial Gods.*
- **Zephyrus** – God of the gentle West Wind and the herald of spring.
- **Zeus** – *See Olympians.*
- **Zodiac** – Spirits of the 12 constellations circling the heavens and measuring the seasons.

Theoi Nomioi – Gods & Beings of the Land

The gods and beings of the countryside, pastures, and wild forests were watched over by Hades, Dionysus, and Artemis.

- **Aegipan** – Goat-footed man who helped Zeus during fight with Typhoeus; placed in the Capricorn constellation.
- **Aix** – Nymph wife of the god Pan.
- **Ampelus** – Young satyr loved by Dionysus; transformed into a vine after death.

- **Anytus** – One of the Curetes (Kuretes) who cared for Despoene.
- **Ariadne** – Wife of Dionysus who helped Theseus slay the Minotaur.
- **Aristaeus** – God of beekeeping, cheese-making, herding, olive-growing and hunting.
- **Artemis** – *See Olympians.*
- **Attis** – Eunuch attendant and consort of Cybele, who drove her lion-drawn chariot across the mountains.
- **Aura** – *See They Might (also) be Titans.*
- **Autonoe** – Wife of the Aristaeus and a nurse of the god Dionysus.
- **Bacchantes / Bassarides** – Thyrsus[76]-wielding women and nymphs who worshiped Dionysus.
- **Britomartis** – Cretan virgin goddess of hunting, fishing, and nets.
- **Cabiri** – Two daemones and orgiastic metalworking gods.
- **Cedalion** – Deity who guided Orion to have his sight restored.
- **Centauri Cyprian** – Horse-bodied men native to Cyprus and devotees of Aphrodite.
- **Centauri Peloponnesian** – Horse-bodied men from Arcadia and Sparta who fought with Herakles.
- **Centauri Thessalian** – Primitive and brutal half-horse men killed after trying to kidnap female wedding guests.
- **Cercopes** – Two monkey-like demi-gods released from capture by Herakles after telling jokes.
- **Chariclo** – Wife of Chiron, daughter of Apollo; possibly a sister of Hecate.
- **Chiron** – Immortal centaur and mentor who lived on Mount Pelion in Thessaly.
- **Comus** – God of festivities and a cup-bearer of Dionysus.
- **Conisalus** – Satyr-like daemon of garden fertility.

- **Corybantes Phrygian** – Daemones who served the Cybele.
- **Corymbus** – Demi-god whose name means 'the fruit of the ivy'.
- **Curetes (Kuretes)** – Daemones who protected Zeus as a baby by hiding him in a cave and making noises to disguise his cries.
- **Cybele** – Mountain goddess who led a pack of lions; worshiped in orgiastic rites.
- **Dactyls**– Five daemones who worked with smelting ore and metal.
- **Dionysus** – *See Olympians.*
- **Dryads** – Nymphs of the trees and forests.
- **Echo** – Nymph who was cursed by Hera to repeat the words of others for the rest of her life.
- **Electra / Elektra** – *See Theoi Halioi / Einalioi – Gods & Beings of the Sea.*
- **Epimelides** – White-haired nymphs of meadows and pastures who guarded sheep and fruit trees.
- **Gaia / Gaea** – *See Primordial Gods.*
- **Hamadyads** – Nymphs of the trees.
- **Hecaerge** – Goddess nymph of archery and companion of Artemis.
- **Hecaterides** – Nymphs of a country dance and mothers of satyrs, Curetes, and Oread nymphs.
- **Hecaterus** – Grandfather of satyrs, Curetes (Kuretes), and mountain nymphs.
- **Hephaestus** – *See Olympians.*
- **Hermes** – *See Olympians.*
- **Loxo** – Archery nymph and companion of Artemis.
- **Maenads / Bacchantes** – Orgiastic female companions of Dionysus.
- **Meliae** – Nymphs of the mountain ash tree, bees, and honey.
- **Melisseus** – Curete (Kurete) of honey and beekeeping.

- **Methe** – Goddess nymph of drunkenness.
- **Nesoi** – *See Primordial Gods.*
- **Nymphs** – *Female nature spirits.*
- **Nysiads** – Nymph nurses of Dionysus.
- **Nysus** – God of Mount Nysa who guarded Dionysus as an infant.
- **Oceanids of Artemis** – 60 young nymphs who followed Artemis.
- **Oreads** – Nymphs of pine trees located on mountains.
- **Orthannes** – Satyr-like fertility daemon.
- **Ourea** – *See Primordial Gods.*
- **Oxylus** – God of mountain forests.
- **Palici** – Daemones of thermal springs and geysers on Sicily.
- **Pan** – God of shepherds and flocks; goat-legged and horned.
- **Panes** – Spirits of the wild with goat legs, horns and tails, and goat-like faces.
- **Phales** – Fertility daemon and satyr god of the processional phallus who followed Dionysus.
- **Pheres Lamian** – Ox-horned, beastly daemones who guarded baby Dionysus.
- **Potami** – Gods of the rivers, often described as man-headed bulls or fish-tailed men.
- **Priapus** – God of garden fertility who has been described as ugly with oversized genitals.
- **Pyrrhichus** – God of the rustic dance.
- **Rhea** – *See Titans.*
- **Satyrs** – Man-like spirits and daemones with horse's-tails, puck-noses and ass's ears.
- **Sileni** – Elderly drunken satyr companions of Dionysus.
- **Silenus** – Elderly, drunken god covered in white hair or fur and nurse of the infant Dionysus.
- **Socus** – Old rustic god native to the island of Euboea.

- **Telete** – Goddess of initiation into the Bacchic orgies.
- **Thriae** – Goddess nymphs of divination by pebbles depicted as women with the bodies of bees.
- **Thyone / Semele** – Mother of Dionysus and a goddess of the Bacchic orgies; killed by Zeus after Hera tricked her; made immortal when Dionysus took her from the underworld.
- **Thysa** – Goddess nymph of the Bacchic frenzy.
- **Tityri** – Flute playing satyrs who followed Dionysus.
- **Tychon** – Fertility god like the satyrs.
- **Upis** – Archer nymph who followed Artemis.
- **Zagreus** – Son of Zeus and Persephone; sometimes described as being resurrected as Dionysus.

Theoi Georgikoi / Khthonioi – Gods & Beings of Agriculture

The gods and beings of the earth or agriculture are placed in the cults of Demeter and Persephone, which also made them part of the Eleusinian mysteries or Theoi Eleusinioi (Eleusinian) and Theoi Mystikoi (Mysteries).

- **Baubo / Iambe** – Eleusinian demi-goddess who helped grief-stricken Demeter laugh with crass jokes and exposed genitalia.
- **Bootes** – Demi-god inventor of the wagon and the plough and son of Demeter; his wagon (Ursa) and himself were memorialized as constellations.
- **Cabiri** – *See Theoi Nomioi – Gods & Beings of the Land.*
- **Cabirides** – Nymphs of the Samothracian Mysteries.
- **Cadmilus** – Father of the Cabiri gods of the Samothracian Mysteries.
- **Calligeneiahe** – Nurse of Demeter or Persephone.
- **Carme** – Goddess-nymph whose name means 'to crop or shear'; daughter of Demeter and Carmanor.

- **Carmanor** – Cretan harvest god (the shearer) and consort of Demeter.
- **Carpi** – Gods of the fruits of the earth described as plump infants.
- **Chrysothemis** – Cretan goddess whose name means 'golden custom'.
- **Cyamites** – Demi-god of the bean (part of the initiatory rites); hero of the Eleusinian Mysteries.
- **Daeira** – *See Chthonian Gods – Gods & Beings of the Underworld.*
- **Demeter** – *See Olympians.*
- **Despoene** – Daughter of the goddess Demeter worshiped in a mystery cult in Arcadia.
- **Dionysus** – *See Olympians.*
- **Dioscuri** – Twin demi-gods (Polydeuces and Castor); mother was Leda but had different fathers.
- **Dysaules** – Demi-god of the Eleusinian Mysteries associated with the field where the first grain was sown.
- **Eleusis** – Oceanid nymph and goddess of the city of Eleusis.
- **Eebouleus** – Eleusinian demi-god connected with plowing and the sowing of seed.
- **Eumolpus** – Eleusinian demi-god whose name means 'fine song'; ancestor of Eleusinian Mysteries priests.
- **Eunostus** – Goddess protector whose names means 'she of the good yield' of the flour mill and the grain silo.
- **Gaia / Gaia** – *See Primordial Gods.*
- **Hades** – *See Chthonian Gods – Gods & Beings of the Underworld.*
- **Hecate / Hekate** – *See They Might (also) be Titans.*
- **Hermes Chthonius** – Guide of the dead who led Persephone back from the underworld in spring.
- **Hestia** – *See Olympians.*
- **Horae / Horai** – *See Minor Olympians.*

- **Iacchus** – God of the ritual cry 'iacche iacche' of Eleusinian processions; led Persephone from the underworld with a torch in his hand.
- **Iasion** – Struck down with a thunderbolt of Zeus for laying with Demeter.
- **Lampades** – *See Chthonian Gods – Gods & Beings of the Underworld.*
- **Macaria** – *See Chthonian Gods – Gods & Beings of the Underworld.*
- **Persephone (Kore)** – *See Chthonian Gods – Gods & Beings of the Underworld.*
- **Plutus** – Blind god of agricultural wealth and bountiful harvests; son of Demeter.
- **Poseidon** – *See Olympians.*
- **Triptolemus** – Hero and demi-god of Eleusis ('he who pounds the husks') commanded by Demeter and Persephone to teach mankind about agriculture.
- **Trochilus** – Demi-god of the Eleusinian Mysteries ('he who turns'); associated with the wheel used for the grinding of flour.
- **Zagreus** – *See Theoi Nomioi – Gods & Beings of the Land.*
- **Zeus** – *See Olympians.*

Chapter 9

Other Beings

The Greek pantheon contains beings, creatures, giants, and more in the stories. This chapter will help you gain some familiarity with other names you might see in myths.

Daemones / Spirits

A daemon is considered a lesser spirit or deity in Greek practice, expanding the range of influence of the gods, as well as providing further nuance into the pantheon. While some names have been mentioned and described, it can be helpful to have them listed separately. Some are listed in Minor Olympians, and it might be wise to remember that one person's definition of a deity or lesser spirit may differ from another's.

It can be helpful to recognize subcategories of daemones (or daimons), including:[77]

- Emotions or feelings, e.g., Love, Hate
- Human experiences, e.g., Death, Poverty
- Qualities, e.g., Beauty, Grace
- Morals, e.g., Hubris, Modesty
- Voices / ways of communicating, e.g., Rumor, Prayer
- Actions / activities, e.g., Murder, Force
- Societal conditions, e.g., Justice, War, Peace

These beings do not necessarily play named roles in a myth, though some do.[78]

- **Achos / Algea** – Pain of Body or Mind, Grief
- **Adephagia** – Gluttony

- **Adicia** – Injustice, Wrongdoing
- **Aedos** – Reverence, Respect
- **Aergia** – Idleness, Laziness
- **Aeschyne** – Shame, Modesty, Honor
- **Aglaea** – Beauty, Splendor, Glory
- **Agon** – Contest, Struggle
- **Alala** – Battle Cry
- **Alastor** – Vengeance
- **Alce** – Courage in Battle
- **Aletheia** – Truth
- **Amechania** – Helplessness
- **Amphilogiae** – Disputes, Debate
- **Anaideia** – Ruthlessness, Shamelessness
- **Anance** – Necessity
- **Androctasiae** – Battle Slaughter
- **Angelia** – Message, Tidings
- **Ania** – Grief, Sorrow, Distress
- **Anteros** – Reciprocated Love
- **Apate** – Trick, Fraud, Deceit, Guile
- **Aporia** – Difficulty, Perplexity
- **Arae** – Curses, Imprecations
- **Arete** – Virtue, Excellence, Goodness
- **Ate** – Delusion, Infatuation,
- **Bia** – Force, Power, Might
- **Cacia** – Vice, Moral Badness
- **Caerus** – Opportunity, Advantage
- **Calleis** – Beauty
- **Calocagathia** – Nobility, Goodness
- **Charis** – Beauty, Grace, Favor
- **Coalemus** – Stupidity, Foolishness
- **Corus** – Satiety, Surfeit, Insolence, Disdain
- **Cratus** – Strength, Might, Power
- **Ctesius** – Home, House

- **Cydoimus** – Confusion, Uproar
- **Deimos / Deimus** – Terror
- **Democracia** – Democracy
- **Dicaiosyne** – Justice, Righteousness
- **Dike** – Justice, Rights
- **Dolus** – Trickery, Craftiness
- **Dysnomia** – Lawlessness
- **Dyssebia** – Impiety
- **Eirene** – Peace
- **Ececheiria** – Truce, Armistice
- **Eleus** – Pity, Mercy, Compassion
- **Elpis** – Hope, Expectation
- **Enyo** – War
- **Epiales** – Nightmare
- **Epidotes** – Ritual Purification
- **Epiphron** – Prudence, Shrewdness
- **Eris** – Rivalry, Strife
- **Eucleia** – Glory
- **Eudaemonia** – Happiness
- **Eunomia** – Civil Order
- **Eupheme** – Praise, Acclamation
- **Euphrosyne** – Cheerfulness, Joy, Mirth
- **Eupraxia** – Good Conduct
- **Eusebia** – Piety, Loyalty
- **Euthenia** – Prosperity, Abundance
- **Euthymia** – Joy, Contentment
- **Eutychia** – Luck, Prosperity, Success
- **Gelus** – Laughter
- **Geras** – Old Age
- **Hedone** – Pleasure, Delight, Sensual Pleasures
- **Hedylogus** – Flattery
- **Hesychia** – Quiet, Rest, Stillness
- **Himerus** – Sexual Desire, Longing, Yearning

- **Homadus** – Battle Noise, Tumult
- **Homonoea** – Unanimity
- **Horcus** – Oath
- **Hormes** – Effort, Eagerness
- **Hybris** – Violence, Excessive Pride
- **Hypnus / Hypnos** – Sleep, Sleepiness
- **Hysminae** – Fighting, Combat
- **Ioke** – Tumult, Pursuit
- **Keres** – Death, Plague
- **Lethe** – Forgetfulness, Oblivion
- **Limus** – Famine, Starvation
- **Litae** – Prayer
- **Lupe** – Pain of Body or Mind, Grief
- **Lyssa** – Rage, Fury, Frenzy
- **Machae** – Battle, Combat
- **Maniae** – Madness, Insanity
- **Methe** – Drunkenness
- **Mnemosyne** – Memory
- **Momus** – Mockery, Ridicule, Blame
- **Morus** – Fate, Destiny, Doom
- **Musica** – Music
- **Neicea** – Quarrel, Feud
- **Nemesis** – Indignation, Jealousy
- **Nomus** – Law, Ordinances
- **Nosi** – Sickness, Disease
- **Oizys** – Woe, Misery
- **Olethrus** – Destruction, Death
- **Oneiri** – Dreams
- **Ossa** – Rumor
- **Palioxis** – Flight, Retreat
- **Paregoros** – Comfort, Consolation
- **Peitharchia** – Obedience
- **Peitho** – Persuasion, Seduction
- **Penia** – Poverty

- **Penthus** – Grief, Sorrow, Mourning
- **Pheme** – Rumor, Gossip, Reputation
- **Philia** – Friendship
- **Philophrosyne** – Friendliness, Welcome
- **Philotes** – Friendship, Love, Affection, Sex
- **Phobus** – Panic, Flight
- **Phoni** – Murder, Slaughter
- **Phrice** – Horror
- **Phthisis** – Perishing, Decay
- **Phthonus** – Envy, Jealousy
- **Phyge** – Escape, Exile, Banishment
- **Pistis** – Trust, Honesty
- **Plutus** – Wealth
- **Poinae** – Retribution, Vengeance, Punishment
- **Polemus** – War, Battle
- **Pompe** – Procession
- **Ponus** – Toil, Labor
- **Porus** – Expediency
- **Praxidicae** – Justice
- **Praxidike** – Justice
- **Proioxis** – Pursuit in Battle
- **Prophasis** – Excuse, Plea
- **Pseudologi** – Lies, Falsehood
- **Ptocheia** – Beggary
- **Sophia** – Wisdom
- **Sophrosyne** – Moderation, Temperance
- **Soter / Soteria** – Safety, Preservation
- **Techne** – Art, Craft
- **Telete** – Consecration, Initiation
- **Thalia** – Festivity, Banquet
- **Thanatus** – Death
- **Thrasus** – Rashness, Insolence
- **Zelus** – Rivalry, Zeal, Ambition

Nymphs

Nymphs, or female spirits, are beings connected to nature and often bound to a particular piece of land.

- **Agyra** – *See Theoi Halioi / Einalioi – Gods & Beings of the Sea.*
- **Aix** – *See Theoi Nomioi – Gods & Beings of the Land.*
- **Anthusae** – Nymphs of flowers.
- **Aurae** – *See Theoi Ouranioi / Meteoroi – Gods & Beings of Sky & Weather.*
- **Automate** – Nymph of a spring in the town of Argos, southern Greece.
- **Autonoe** – One of the 50 Nereids.
- **Bacchae / Epimelides** – Bacchic nymphs and companions of Dionysus.
- **Baccantes / Bassarides** – *See Theoi Nomioi – Gods & Beings of the Land.*
- **Benthesicyme** – *See Theoi Halioi / Einalioi – Gods & Beings of the Sea.*
- **Cabeiro** – *See Theoi Halioi / Einalioi – Gods & Beings of the Sea.*
- **Cabirides** – *See Theoi Georgikoi / Khthonioi – Gods & Beings of Agriculture.*
- **Calliste** – *See Theoi Halioi / Einalioi – Gods & Beings of the Sea.*
- **Calypso** – Goddess nymph of the island of Ogygia.
- **Capheira** – *See Theoi Halioi / Einalioi – Gods & Beings of the Sea.*
- **Carme** – *See Theoi Georgikoi / Khthonioi – Gods & Beings of Agriculture.*
- **Crenaeae** – Nymphs of wells and fountains.
- **Cymopoleia** – *See Theoi Halioi / Einalioi – Gods & Beings of the Sea.*

- **Daerira** – *See Chthonian Gods – Gods & Beings of the Underworld.*
- **Daphne** – Nymph loved by Apollo, but she escaped his embrace by transforming into a laurel tree.
- **Dione** – *See They Might (also) be Titans.*
- **Dryads** – *See Theoi Nomioi – Gods & Beings of the Land.*
- **Echo** – *See Theoi Nomioi – Gods & Beings of the Land.*
- **Electra / Elektra** – *See Theoi Halioi / Einalioi – Gods & Beings of the Sea.*
- **Eleusis** – *See Theoi Georgikoi / Khthonioi – Gods & Beings of Agriculture.*
- **Epimelides** – *See Theoi Nomioi – Gods & Beings of the Land.*
- **Eurynome** – *See they Might (also) be Titans.*
- **Gorgyra** – *See Chthonian Gods – Gods & Beings of the Underworld.*
- **Haliae** – *See Theoi Halioi / Einalioi – Gods & Beings of the Sea.*
- **Hamadryads** – *See Theoi Nomioi – Gods & Beings of the Land.*
- **Heleionomae** – Nymphs of freshwater marshes and wetlands.
- **Helle** – *See Theoi Halioi / Einalioi – Gods & Beings of the Sea.*
- **Hyades** – *See Theoi Ouranioi / Meteoroi – Gods & Beings of Sky & Weather.*
- **Io** – Naiad[79] disguised as a heifer so Zeus could be with her, but Hera found out and plagued Io with a gadfly that caused Io to wander to Egypt.
- **Lampades** – *See Chthonian Gods – Gods & Beings of the Underworld.*
- **Leimenides** – *See Theoi Halioi / Einalioi – Gods & Beings of the Sea.*
- **Leuce** – *See Chthonian Gods – Gods & Beings of the Underworld.*

- **Loxo** – *See Theoi Nomioi – Gods & Beings of the Land.*
- **Maenads** – *See Theoi Nomioi – Gods & Beings of the Land.*
- **Meliades** – Nymphs of highland pasture; protectresses of flocks of sheep.
- **Meliae / Melissae** – *See Theoi Nomioi – Gods & Beings of the Land.*
- **Menae** – *See Theoi Ouranioi / Meteoroi – Gods & Beings of Sky & Weather.*
- **Methe** – *See Theoi Nomioi – Gods & Beings of the Land.*
- **Metis** – *See they Might (also) be Titans.*
- **Minthe** – *See Chthonian Gods – Gods & Beings of the Underworld.*
- **Naiads** – *See Theoi Halioi / Einalioi – Gods & Beings of the Sea.*
- **Nephelae** – *See Theoi Ouranioi / Meteoroi – Gods & Beings of Sky & Weather.*
- **Nereids** – *See Theoi Halioi / Einalioi – Gods & Beings of the Sea.*
- **Nesoi** – *See Primordial Gods.*
- **Nysiads** – *See Theoi Nomioi – Gods & Beings of the Land.*
- **Oceanids** – *See Theoi Halioi / Einalioi – Gods & Beings of the Sea.*
- **Oceanids of Artemis** – *See Theoi Nomioi – Gods & Beings of the Land.*
- **Oeolyca** – *See Theoi Halioi / Einalioi – Gods & Beings of the Sea.*
- **Oreads** – *See Theoi Nomioi – Gods & Beings of the Land.*
- **Orphne** – *See Chthonian Gods – Gods & Beings of the Underworld.*
- **Pallas** – *See they Might (also) be Titans.*
- **Pegaeae** – Nymphs of springs.
- **Pleiades** – *See Theoi Ouranioi / Meteoroi – Gods & Beings of Sky & Weather.*

- **Potameides** – Nymphs of the rivers.
- **Rhode** – *See Theoi Halioi / Einalioi – Gods & Beings of the Sea.*
- **Sirens** – *See Theoi Halioi / Einalioi – Gods & Beings of the Sea.*
- **Styx** – *See Primordial Gods.*
- **Thoosa** – *See Theoi Halioi / Einalioi – Gods & Beings of the Sea.*
- **Thriae** – *See Theoi Nomioi – Gods & Beings of the Land.*
- **Thyiads** – Wild, orgiastic nymphs who worshiped Dionysus; known as Maenads, Bacchae, and Bacchantes.
- **Thysa** – *See Theoi Nomioi – Gods & Beings of the Land.*
- **Triteia** – *See Theoi Halioi / Einalioi – Gods & Beings of the Sea.*
- **Upis** – *See Theoi Nomioi – Gods & Beings of the Land.*
- **Urania** – One of the Oceanid nymphs.

Creatures

Within Greek stories are mythical creatures, including monsters, animals, dragons, giants, ghosts, and more.

- **Achlys** – Daemon of misery and pale green hag with bleeding cheeks, tear-stained eyes, long fingernails, and dusty hair.
- **Aegipan** – *See Theoi Nomioi – Gods & Beings of the Land.*
- **Amphisbaena** – Serpent with two heads, one at each end of its body.
- **Ants** – Gigantic ants which guarded gold fields.
- **Automotons** – Lifelike statues or creatures crafted by Hephaestus out of metal.
- **Basiliscs** – Deadly serpents which are killed by touch.
- **Birds of Ares** – Arrow-shooting birds which guarded a shrine of Ares.

- **Birds, Stymphalian** – Man-eating birds that Herakles was sent to drive away as one of his labors.
- **Boar, Crommyonian** – Gigantic sow slain by Theseus.
- **Boar, Erymanthian** – Arcadian boar that Herakles fetched as one of his twelve labors.
- **Bulls, Bronze** – Four fire-breathing, bronze bulls Hephaestus crafted for King Aeetes of Colchis.
- **Bull, Cretan** – Bull which impregnated the Pasiphae queen of Crete, and Herakles collected as one of his labors.
- **Catoblepas** – Bull-like African beast whose downward looking head, when raised, could kill a man with a gaze or with its noxious breath.
- **Centaurs / Centauri** – Tribe of creatures with the heads and torsos of men and the bodies of horses.
- **Cerberus** – *See Chthonian Gods – Gods & Beings of the Underworld.*
- **Cetea, Indian** – Half-animal, half-fish sea-monster.
- **Chimera** – Three-headed monster with the front of a lion, the hind-parts of a goat and goat's head rising from its back, and the tail of a headed-serpent.
- **Chiron** – *See Theoi Nomioi – Gods & Beings of the Land.*
- **Crab, Giant (Carcinus)** – *See Theoi Halioi / Einalioi – Gods & Beings of the Sea.*
- **Crocotta / Leucrocotae** – Hyena-like with a powerful jaw-plate in place of teeth; imitated the human voice to lure prey.
- **Deer, Cerynitian** – Golden-horned deer Herakles was sent to find as one of his twelve labors.
- **Deer, Golden-Horned** – Five immortal golden-horned deer sacred to the goddess Artemis.
- **Dracaenae** – Female-monsters with the heads and torsos of women and serpentine-tails in place of leg.
- **Dragons** – Giant, toothed serpentine monsters.

- **Eagle** – Eagle which fed on the liver of Prometheus.
- **Eale** – Antelope-like beast with tusks and moveable horns.
- **Echidna** – *See Theoi Halioi / Einalioi – Gods & Beings of the Sea.*
- **Fox, Teumessian** – Gigantic fox that preyed upon children in Thebes.
- **Glaucus** – *See Theoi Halioi / Einalioi – Gods & Beings of the Sea.*
- **Gorgons** – *See Theoi Halioi / Einalioi – Gods & Beings of the Sea.*
- **Graeae** – *See Theoi Halioi / Einalioi – Gods & Beings of the Sea.*
- **Griffins** – Winged beasts with the heads of eagles and the bodies of lions.
- **Harpies / Harpyie** – *See Theoi Halioi / Einalioi – Gods & Beings of the Sea.*
- **Horses** – Breed of swift-footed, immortal horses.
- **Lion, Nemean** – Gigantic lion whose skin was impervious to weapons; strangled by Herakles.
- **Maidens, Golden** – Gour golden maidens which Hephaestus crafted as his own attendants.
- **Manticore** – Winged monster with a man's head, a lion's body, and a spiked missile-throwing tail.
- **Medusa** – Mortal Gorgon slain by Perseus.
- **Minotaur** – Cretan monster with a bill head and the hairy body of a man.
- **Monocerata / Unicorns** – Unicorns; magical single-horned equines native to India.
- **Neades** – Giant beast whose roar could split the ground open.
- **Onocentaur** – African animal with features of a man and an ass.
- **Panes** – *See Theoi Nomioi – Gods & Beings of the Land.*

- **Pegasus** – Winged horse ridden into battle with the Chimera.
- **Phasma** – Ghosts or phantoms, some with bodies and some were body-less.
- **Phoenix** – Golden-red bird whose feathers shone with the light of the sun.
- **Ram, Golden-Fleeced** – Flying, talking, golden-fleeced ram who rescued Phrixus and Helle.
- **Satyrs** – *See Theoi Nomioi – Gods & Beings of the Land.*
- **Scolopendra** – Sea-monster with long nose hair; flat, crayfish-like tail and rows of webbed feet on flanks.
- **Scorpion** – Scorpion sent to slay the giant Orion.
- **Scylla** – *See Theoi Halioi / Einalioi – Gods & Beings of the Sea.*
- **Serpents, Winged** – Feathery-winged serpents of Arabia which guarded the valuable myrrh fields.
- **Sphinx** – Theban monster with the head of a woman and the body of a lioness.
- **Talos** – Bronze giant Hephaestus crafted for Queen Europa of Crete to patrol her island borders.
- **Triton** – *See Theoi Halioi / Einalioi – Gods & Beings of the Sea.*
- **Yale** – Antelope-like beast with tusks and moveable horns.

Giants

Oversized men were the Giants in Greek stories and myths and were often closely connected to the gods.

- **Agrius** – Man-eating Thracian giant who was half man and half bear.
- **Alcyoneus** – King of the Thracian giants who was slain by Herakles.

- **Aloadae** – Twin giants who attempted to enter heaven by piling mountains on each other.
- **Alpos** – Sicilian giant slain by Dionysus.
- **Anax** – Lydian Giant.
- **Antaeus** – Libyan king who wrestled all visitors to death until he was slain by Herakles.
- **Antiphates** – King of the man-eating giants known as Laestrygones encountered by Odysseus.
- **Arges** – One of the three elder Cyclopes.
- **Argos Panoptes** – Hundred-eyed giant sent by Hera to guard the maiden Io but was slain by Hermes.
- **Aristaeus** – One of the Thracian Gigantes transformed into a dung beetle when he fled the battle with the gods.
- **Asterius** – Lydian giant.
- **Azeus** – Arcadian giant who fought in the War of the Titans.
- **Briareus** – *See they Might (also) be Titans.*
- **Brontes** – One of the three elder Cyclopes who forged the lightning bolts of Zeus.
- **Cacus** – Fire-breathing giant slain by Herakles.
- **Charybdis** – *See Theoi Halioi / Einalioi – Gods & Beings of the Sea.*
- **Chrysaor** – Giant born from the neck of the beheaded Medusa.
- **Cottus** – One of the three hundred-handed Hecatoncheires.
- **Cyclopes** – *See They Might (also) be Titans.*
- **Cymopoleia** – Gigantic daughter of Poseidon who wed the hundred-handed giant Briareus.
- **Damasen** – Mysian giant who destroyed a dragon.
- **Damysus** – Swiftest of the Thracian Gigantes who made war on the gods.
- **Echidnades** – Serpent-footed giant and ally of the Titans; slain by Ares.

- **Elatreus** – Giant son of one of the elder Cyclopes who was slain by Apollo.
- **Enceladus** – One of the Thracian Gigantes who made war on the gods; buried by the goddess Athena.
- **Ephialtes** – One of the twin giants (Aloadae) who attempted to storm heaven.
- **Euryalus** – One of the sons of the three elder Cyclopes slain by Apollo.
- **Eurymedon** – King of the giants who led his people to ruin.
- **Gegenees** – Tribe of six armed giants encountered and slain by the Argonauts.
- **Geryon** – Three-bodied giant slain by Herakles as one of his twelve labors.
- **Gigantes** – 100 Thracian giants born of Gaia after impregnated by the blood of the castrated Uranus.
- **Gyes** – One of the hundred-handed Hecatoncheires.
- **Halimedes** – Son of one of three elder Cyclopes slain by Apollo to avenge the death of Asclepius.
- **Hecatoncheires** – *See They Might (also) be Titans.*
- **Hoplodamus** – Warrior giant who helped Rhea after Cronus learned of her hiding of the infant Zeus.
- **Hyllus** – Lydian Giant.
- **Hyperborean Giants** – Three giant sons of Boreas.
- **Laestrygones** – Cannibalistic giants encountered by Odysseus on his travels.
- **Leon** – One of the Thracian Gigantes who fought the gods; slain by Herakles.
- **Mylinus** – Cretan giant slain by Zeus.
- **Oeolyca** – Daughter of Briareus.
- **Olympus** – Cretan giant who mentored Zeus.
- **Oreus** – Man-eating Thracian giant who was half-man and half-bear.

- **Orion** – Hunter who could walk on water; slain and placed amongst the stars as a constellation.
- **Otus** – One of the twin giants (Aloadae).
- **Periboea** – Daughter of the king of the giants.
- **Polybotes** – One of the Thracian giants buried beneath an island by Poseidon.
- **Polyphemus** – Cannibalistic Cyclops blinded by Odysseus.
- **Porphyrion** – Thracian Gigante who attempted to rape Hera in the war but was destroyed by Herakles and Zeus with arrows and lightning bolts.
- **Rhodian Gigantes** – Race of giants native to the island of Rhodes.
- **Steropes** – One of the three elder cyclopes who forged the lightning bolts of Zeus.
- **Syceus** – One of the Thracian Gigantes who fought the gods; fled and was transformed into a fig tree.
- **Talos** – Giant molded out of bronze to patrol Crete; slain by the Medea when he tried to prevent the Argonauts from landing.
- **Tityus** – Giant slain by Apollo and Artemis when he attempted to violate their mother Leto.
- **Trachius** – Gigantic son of one of the elder Cyclopes slain by the god Apollo.
- **Typhoeus / Typhon** – Winged giant with man-like features from the waist up, two serpents instead of legs, serpent heads for fingers.

Still More Figures to Know

The more you read the Greek myths, the more you will find important humans.

- **Achilles** – Great hero of the Trojan War, a son of Peleus and Thetis.
- **Actaeon** – Hunter who spied Artemis bathing and transformed into a stag and torn apart by his hounds.
- **Adonis** – Handsome youth loved by Aphrodite killed by a boar while hunting alone.
- **Andromeda** – Ethiopian princess chained to the rocks as a sacrifice for the sea-monster ravaging the coast; rescued and married to Perseus.
- **Arachne** – Weaver who challenged Athena to a weaving contest and was turned into a spider.
- **Callisto** – Arcadian princess and hunting companion of Artemis; loved by Zeus, but was turned into a bear when her pregnancy was revealed.
- **Diomedes of Thrace** – King of the Thracian Bistones who fed human flesh to his mares; slain by Herakles sent to fetch the horses as one of his twelve labors.
- **Ganymede** – Handsome Trojan prince carried to heaven by Zeus in the guise of an eagle; became the cupbearer of the gods.
- **Herakles / Heracles** – Great hero who completed the twelve labors assigned by King Eurystheus.
- **Hippolyte** – Queen of the Amazons, whose belt Herakles was sent to fetch as one of his twelve labors; she was killed by the hero.
- **Jason** – Hero who led the Argonauts to find the Golden Fleece; won Medea for his bride in a contest.
- **Midas** – King of Phrygia who entertained Silenus when he became separated from the god's company; rewarded with a golden touch.
- **Minyades** – Three princesses of Orchomenus who scorned the worship of Dionysus; driven mad and dismembered one of their sons before being changed into owls and bats.

- **Narcissus** – Arrogant youth who spurned the attention of others and cursed to fall in love with his own reflection; transformed into a daffodil.
- **Odysseus** – Hero of the Trojan War, whose fleet was blown off course in a storm and took ten years to return home to his wife, Penelope.
- **Oedipus** – Hero who destroyed the Sphinx and was crowned King of Thebes; unintentionally killed his father and married his mother.
- **Pandora** – First woman created by the gods; delivered evil to man when she opened a box/jar of harmful spirits.
- **Perseus** – Commanded to fetch the Gorgon's head; returned with the head and turned the king to stone.
- **Psyche** – Challenged by Aphrodite for loving Eros; made immortal.
- **Pygmalion** – Cypriot king who fell in love with an ivory statue; Aphrodite brought the statue to life.
- **Theseus** – Athenian hero who slayed the Minotaur.

With so many beings and figures in ancient Greek myths, it becomes clear how the concept of deity interacted with the world on many levels. Every part of life had the influence of the mystical and magical, and thus every part of life could be blessed and known as divine.

Conclusion

> Scepticism is as much the result of knowledge, as knowledge is of scepticism. To be content with what we at present know, is, for the most part, to shut our ears against conviction; since, from the very gradual character of our education, we must continually forget, and emancipate ourselves from, knowledge previously acquired; we must set aside old notions and embrace fresh ones; and, as we learn, we must be daily unlearning something which it has cost us no small labour and anxiety to acquire.
>
> Introduction by Theodore Alois Buckley for Homer, *The Odyssey*, translated by Alexander Pope[80]

While it might be unexpected to end a book about Greek mythology with the idea of skepticism, if these gods have taught me anything, it's to ask more questions. With each reading of a myth and each new book or resource I found, the gods became more complex, even if the facts were similar in tone and content. But isn't that the way humans are too? Though we might desire to be easy to see and understand, we aren't. We never will be. And that is a gift to be alive and unfolding in each moment, perhaps harder to know, but also wiser in the nuance of being perceived and interpreted.

What lives on in myth, lives on in life. I walk in this world with a healthy dose of disbelief, the kind that allows me to stay curious, open, and willing to be proven wrong. To be proven unable to see things as beautiful as they truly are. But with the hope I will continue to look and look again. This is the magick for me, the magick of possibility and influence and evolution.

I thank the deities of beginning and creation:

Gaia, thank you for your birthing,
Nyx, thank you for the dark shadow of possibility,
Chronos, thank you for the time to know and to act,
Eros, thank you for the boundlessness of creation,
Oceanus, thank you for the flow and the waters that stretch to all horizons,
Thalassa, thank you for the wonder of the sea,
Ananke, thank you for bringing necessity,
Hemera, thank you for reminding us the day will come again,
Ourea, thank you for the sharpness of mountains to carry the edges,
Pontus, thank you for the width of the seas,
Tethys, thank you for holding us and nourishing us,
Uranus, thank you for the curve of sky.

I thank the deities that became the elders and the banished:

Coeus, thank you for the power of intellect,
Crius, thank you for the brightness of constellations,
Cronus, thank you for the lesson of sharp harvests,
Hyperion, thank you for the measure of time and light,
Iapetus, thank you for the reminder of mortality,
Mnemosyne, thank for the power of memory and recollection,
Oceanus, thank you for the waters of never-ending time,
Phoebe, thank you for the reminder of prophecy's power,
Rhea, thank you for the cunningness that saved your child,
Tethys, thank you for nursing life with fresh waters,
Theia, thank you for the gifts of sight and knowing
Themis, thank you for your advice to the gods about order and tradition.

I thank the Olympians, whose names are known and repeated as the victorious and the complicated:

Aphrodite, thank you for your love and beauty,
Apollo, thank you for places of healing and knowing,
Ares, thank you for strength and doing what is needed,
Artemis, thank you for calling the wild back to us,
Athena, thank you for knowing yourself and claiming yourself,
Demeter, thank you for your determination and your willingness to travel to the ends of it all,
Dionysus, thank you for reminding us of joy and ecstasy,
Hephaestus, thank you for being a sharp tool of discernment,
Hera, thank you for teaching us of resilience and right-sized anger,
Hermes, thank you for carrying what we need to hear and know,
Hestia, thank you for warming the halls and bringing community together,
Poseidon, thank you for showing the powers of destruction,
Zeus, thank you for lessons of stepping into the complicated place of leadership and power.

Within your histories lie greatness and tragedy, within your words are magick and wisdom, within your halls, may this short book honor you.

May those who seek to know you find what they seek.
May those who speak your names remember their power too.
May those who place offerings in your temples know their divinity too.

Many blessings on the journeys you take. May they bring you to the places that know your name and sing you alive across the ages.

Appendix A – Terms

Ancient Greece – The phrase used to describe the area in which Greek mythology began, though a challenging phrase because the culture and the people varied in social structure, religious practices, deities worshiped, and more.

Chthonian – Used to describe the gods who were a part of the underworld and who engaged with death and the dead.

Daemones / Daimones – Lesser deities or spirits.

Demi-gods – Beings born of a mortal and a deity, or a mortal given the powers of a deity but with lesser divine status.

Epithet – Adjective or descriptor that includes a quality or attribute for a deity or being.

Giants – Large and aggressive beings who were often feared for their strength.

Hellenism – The imitation of practices from ancient Greece.

Mystery Cults – Groups that offer mystical experiences and secret rites outside of the public rituals and practices; often dedicated to a certain god or goddess.

Nymphs – Female-boded spirits who were associated with fertility and nature.

Olympians – Deities that ruled after winning the War of the Titans, including Aphrodite, Apollo, Ares, Artemis, Athena, Demeter, Dionysus, Hera, Hermes, Hephaestus, Hestia, Poseidon, and Zeus.

Primordial / Primeval Deities – Deities at the beginning of time who created the Titans.

Satyr – Creature with a human body and lion's head.

Theoi – Greek word for gods or deities.

Titans – Deities who came after the primordial gods, including Coeus, Crius, Cronos, Hyperion, Iapetus, Mnemosyne, Oceanus, Phoebe, Rhea, Tethys, Theia, and Themis.

Appendix B – Recommended Reading

Albert, Liv. *Greek Mythology: The Gods, Goddesses, and Heroes Handbook*. Adams Media. 2021.

Apollodorus. *The Library of Greek Mythology*. Translated by J.G. Frazer. Oxford University Press. 2017.

Apollodorus. *The Library of Greek Mythology*. Translated by Robin Hard. Oxford University Press. 1997.

Athanassakis, Apostolos N. *Theogony, Works and Days*. Shield. Johns Hopkins University Press. 1983

Baring, Anne and Jules Cashford. *The Myth of the Goddess*. Penguin Books.1993.

Batchelor, Stephen. *The Ancient Greeks for Dummies*. For Dummies. 2011.

Bingham, Jane. *The World of Mythology: Classical Myth, A Treasury of Greek and Roman Legends, Art, and History*. Sharpe Focus. 2008.

Bolen, Jean Shinoda, MD. *Goddesses in Everywoman: Powerful Archetypes in Women's Lives*. HarperCollins. 1984.

Bolten, Lesley. *The Everything Classical Mythology Book*. F+W Publications 2002.

Bryant, Megan E. *Mytholopedia – Oh My Gods! A Look-It-Up Guide to the Gods of Mythology*. Scholastic. 2010.

Buxton, Richard. *Greek Myths & Tales: Epic Tales*. Flame Tree Collections. 2018.

Carabas, Markus and Charles River Editors. *Magic in Ancient Greece: The History and Legacy of the Religious Rituals Practiced by the Greeks*. Charles River Editors. 2016.

Connelly, Joan Breton. *Portrait of a Priestess: Women and Ritual in Ancient Greece*. Princeton University Press. 2007.

Due, Casey and Mary Ebbott. *Iliad 10 and the Poetics of Ambush: A Multitext Edition with Essays and Commentary*. Harvard University Press. 2011.

Evslin, Bernard. *Gods, Demigods, and Demons: An Encyclopedia of Greek Mythology*. Scholastic Inc. 1975.

Fantham, Elaine, Helene Peet Foley, Natalie Noymel Kampen, Sarah B. Pomeroy, and H. Alan Shapiro. *Women in the Classical World*. Oxford University Press. 1994.

Fransman, Karrie and Jonathan Plackett. *Gender Swapped Greek Myths*. Faber & Faber. 2022.

Freeman, Philip. *Oh My Gods: A Modern Retelling of Greek and Roman Myths*. Simon & Schuster Paperbacks. 2012.

Goodrich, Norma Lorre. *Priestesses*. Harper Perennial. 1989.

Graves, Robert. *The Greek Myths*. Penguin Books 1993.

Grimal, Pierre. *The Penguin Dictionary of Classical Mythology*. Penguin Books, 1991.

Haynes, Natalie. *Pandora's Jar: Women in Greek Myths*. Harper Perennial. 2022.

Hesiod. *Theogony*. Translated by M.L. West. Oxford University Press. 1988.

Higgins, Charlotte. *Greek Myths: A New Retelling*. Pantheon. 2022.

Homer. *The Iliad*. Translated by Emily Wilson. W.W. Norton & Company. 2023.

Homer. *The Odyssey*. Translated by Emily Wilson. W.W. Norton & Company. 2017.

Hope, Murry. *Practical Greek Magic*. The Aquarian Press. 1985.

Impelluso, Lucia. *Myths: Tales of the Greek and Roman Gods*. Abrams. 2008.

Jackson, J.L, editor. *Greek Myths & Legends: Tales of Heroes, Gods & Monsters*. Flame Tree Publishing. 2022.

Johnston, Sarah Iles. *Gods and Mortals: Ancient Greek Myths for Modern Readers*. Princeton University Press. 2023.

Lattimore, Richmond. *The Iliad of Homer*. The University of Chicago Press. 2011.

Lefkowitz, Mary. *Greek Gods, Human Lives: What We Can Learn from Myths*. Yale University Press. 2003.

Lefkowitz, Mary R. *Women in Greek Myth*, Second Edition. The Johns Hopkins University Press. 1986, 2007.

Lightman, Marjorie and Benjamin Lightman. *Ancient Greek & Roman Women*. Checkmark Books. 2000.

Lizos, George. *Secrets of Greek Mysticism: A Modern Guide to Daily Practice with the Greek Gods and Goddesses*. Hampton Roads Publishing. 2024.

Mankey, Jason & Astrea Taylor. *Modern Witchcraft with the Greek Gods: History, Insights & Magickal Practice*. Llewellyn Publications. 2022.

Mascetti, Manuela Dunn. *Aphrodite: Goddess of Love – Goddess Wisdom*. Chronicle Books. 1996.

Matyszak, Philip. *The Gods and Goddesses of Greece & Rome*. Thames & Hudson. 2022.

Miller, Madeline. *Circe*. Little, Brown & Company. 2018.

Monaghan, Patricia. *The New Book of Goddesses & Heroines*. Llewellyn Publications. 1997.

Moon, Irisanya. *Pagan Portals – Aphrodite: Encountering the Goddess of Love and Beauty and Initiation*. Moon Books, 2020.

Moon, Irisanya. *Pagan Portals – Artemis: Goddess of the Wild Hunt and Sovereign Heart*. Moon Books. 2024.

Moon, Irisanya. *Earth Spirit – Gaia: Saving Her, Saving Ourselves*. Moon Books. 2023.

Moon, Irisanya. *Pagan Portals – Iris: Goddess of the Rainbow and Messenger of the Godds*. Moon Books. 2021.

Ostwald, Martin. *Language and History in Ancient Greek Culture*. University of Pennsylvania Press. 2009.

Parin D'aulaires, Ingri and Edgar. *D'aulaires' Book of Greek Myths*. Bantam Doubleday Dell Publishing Group. 1962.

Paris, Ginette. Pagan Meditations: *The Worlds of Aphrodite, Artemis, and Hestia*. Spring Publications, Inc. 1986.

Pomeroy, Sarah B. *Goddesses, Whores, Wives, and Slaves: Women in Classical Antiquity*. Schocken Books. 1975.

Powell, Barry B. *Greek Poems to the Gods: Hymns from Home to Proclus*. University of California Press. 2021.

Rayor, Diane J. *The Homeric Hymns: A Translation, with Introduction and Notes*. University of California Press. 2014.

Roberts, Ellie Mackin. *Heroines of Olympus: The Women of Greek Mythology*. Welbeck. 2020.

Rose. H.J. *A Handbook of Greek Mythology*. E.P. Dutton & Co., Inc. 1959.

Trzaskoma Stephen M., Scott R. Smith, and Stephen Brunet. *Anthology of Classical Myth: Primary Sources in Translation*. Hackett Publishing Company. 2016.

Vernant, Jean-Pierre. *The Universe, The Gods, and Men*. HarperCollins Publishers. 2001.

Wasson, R. Gordon, Albert Hofmann, and Carl A. P. Ruck. *The Road to Eleusis: Unveiling the Secret of the Mysteries*. North Atlantic Books. 2008.

Weigle, Marta. *Spiders & Spinsters: Women and Mythology*. University of New Mexico Press. 1982.

Resources on Sexual Violence in Greek Mythology

https://academic.oup.com/book/774/chapter-abstract/135416726?redirectedFrom=fulltext

https://www.cram.com/essay/Rape-In-Ancient-Greek-Mythology/FJFXZSWAK4T

https://erickimphotography.com/blog/2024/03/10/what-does-rape-mean-in-classical-greek-roman-context/

https://bora.uib.no/bora-xmlui/bitstream/handle/1956/19935/HIS350-7.pdf?sequence=1&isAllowed=y

https://womeninantiquity.wordpress.com/2017/12/06/consent-and-rape-culture-in-ancient-greece/

https://www.jhiblog.org/2019/05/06/a-rape-by-any-other-name-against-teaching-abductions-in-greek-art-2/

https://feminisminindia.com/2017/10/06/origins-rape-culture-mythology/

https://foundinantiquity.com/2013/10/06/rape-culture-in-classical-mythology/

https://classicalwisdom.com/mythology/gods/the-rape-of-a-goddess/

https://educationispowerful.net/greek-mythology-and-me-too/

https://sententiaeantiquae.com/2023/07/09/sexual-violence-in-ancient-myth/

https://classics.domains.skidmore.edu/lit-campus-only/secondary/Lefkowitz%201994.pdf

Baring, Anne and Jules Cashford. *The Myth of the Goddess*. Penguin Books.1993.

Connelly, Joan Breton. *Portrait of a Priestess: Women and Ritual in Ancient Greece*. Princeton University Press. 2007.

Fantham, Elaine, Helene Peet Foley, Natalie Noymel Kampen, Sarah B. Pomeroy, and H. Alan Shapiro. *Women in the Classical World*. Oxford University Press. 1994.

Goodrich, Norma Lorre. *Priestesses*. Harper Perennial. 1989.

Haynes, Natalie. *Pandora's Jar: Women in Greek Myths*. Harper Perennial. 2022.

Lefkowitz, Mary R. *Women in Greek Myth*, Second Edition. The Johns Hopkins University Press. 1986, 2007.

Lightman, Marjorie and Benjamin Lightman. *Ancient Greek & Roman Women*. Checkmark Books. 2000.

Paris, Ginette. *Pagan Meditations: The Worlds of Aphrodite, Artemis, and Hestia*. Spring Publications, Inc. 1986.

Pomeroy, Sarah B. *Goddesses, Whores, Wives, and Slaves: Women in Classical Antiquity*. Schocken Books. 1975.

Endnotes

1. https://charlesloder.github.io/greekTransliteration/
2. Sometimes referred to as Hellenismos, or "Unadapted borrowing from Ancient Greek Ἑλληνισμός (Ellēnismós, "imitation of the Greeks")" from https://en.wiktionary.org/wiki/Hellenismos
3. Morris, Ian and Powell, Barry. *The Greeks: History, Culture, and Society*. p 13.
4. https://www.artnews.com/art-news/news/greek-gods-sculptures-heads-found-aizanoi-turkey-1234676114/
5. Basic Ancient Greece map, created by Irisanya Moon, with https://www.deviantart.com/thegreatlocust/art/Blank-map-of-Greece-and-the-Aegean-Sea-730186664 (free to use, no need to ask for permission)
6. Budin, Stephanie Lynn. *The Ancient Greeks: An Introduction*. p 3.
7. https://en.wikipedia.org/wiki/History_of_Greece
8. https://www.worldhistory.org/Mycenaean_Civilization/
9. Sansone, David. *Ancient Greek Civilization*. p 58.
10. https://www.britannica.com/place/ancient-Greece
11. Hesiod was the author of *Theogony* and *Works and Days*, which recounted stories of deities and the everyday person. This will be described in more detail in later chapters.
12. https://bora.uib.no/bora-xmlui/bitstream/handle/1956/19935/HIS350-7.pdf?sequence=1&isAllowed=y
13. https://soar.suny.edu/bitstream/handle/20.500.12648/1873/Alwang_Honors.pdf?sequence=1&isAllowed=y
14. https://classics.domains.skidmore.edu/lit-campus-only/secondary/Lefkowitz%201994.pdf
15. https://wist.info/sophocles/46686/
16. https://www.merriam-webster.com/dictionary/mythology
17. https://www.britannica.com/topic/Greek-mythology

18. https://chs.harvard.edu/chapter/part-i-introduction-to-homeric-poetry/#:~:text=Homeric%20poetry%20is%20a%20cover,the%20epic%20of%20the%20Odyssey
19. Budin, Stephanie Lynn. *The Ancient Greeks*. p 404.
20. Palaima, Thomas G. *Linear B Sources, located in Appendix One in Anthology of Classical Myth: Primary Sources in Translation*, Second Edition.
21. https://en.wikipedia.org/wiki/Derveni_papyrus
22. https://chs.harvard.edu/derveni-papyrus-introduction/
23. https://chs.harvard.edu/publications-projects-derveni/
24. https://www.britannica.com/topic/Greek-mythology/Forms-of-myth-in-Greek-culture
25. https://chs.harvard.edu/curated-article/gregory-nagy-lyric-and-greek-myth/
26. https://wcc-uk.blogs.sas.ac.uk/resources/classical-translations-and-editions-by-women/
27. https://www.oxfordreference.com/display/10.1093/oi/authority.20110803095641467
28. https://www.oxfordreference.com/display/10.1093/oi/authority.20110803095641437
29. https://science.jrank.org/pages/10928/Pythagoreanism-Number-Cosmos-Harmony.html#:~:text=Pythagoras%20was%20the%20first%20person,embody%20geometrical%20form%20and%20proportion.
30. https://www.merriam-webster.com/dictionary/cosmogony
31. The war between the Titans and the eventual Olympians.
32. The Truth and the Falsehood of Myths – Scientific Figure on ResearchGate. Available to use with attribution: https://www.researchgate.net/figure/A-universe-consisting-of-three-storeys-17_fig1_343577760 [accessed 17 Jun, 2024],
33. Goddesses of the seasons, or Hôra / Hôrai
34. Charon / Karon was the ferryman who waited at the boat and took a coin from the soul in exchange for the journey.
35. Hundred-handed giants and sons of Gaia and Uranus.

36. Kantor, Uriel. *Ancient Greek Cosmology: How Did the Greeks See the Universe?*. 2023. Retrieved from https://www.thecollector.com/cosmology-ancient-greece/
37. Milic, Anja. *Anaximander 101: An Exploration of His Metaphysics*. 2021. Retrieved from https://www.thecollector.com/anaximander-greek-philosopher/
38. https://www.thoughtco.com/aristarchus-of-samos-3072223
39. Barbette, Stanley Spaeth. *The Cambridge companion to ancient Mediterranean religions*. 2013.
40. Eubulus. *Semele or Dionysus,* fr. 93. preserved in Athenaeus, *Deipnosophists* 2.37c
41. Connelly, Joan Breton. *Portrait of a Priestess: Women and Ritual in Ancient Greece*.
42. https://www.atlasobscura.com/articles/the-ancient-greeks-sacrificed-ugly-people
43. https://archive.chs.harvard.edu/CHS/article/display/3963.8-the-oath-in-greece
44. https://en.wikipedia.org/wiki/Marriage_in_ancient_Greece#:~:text=were%20called%20parthenioi.-,Marriage%20celebration,was%20the%20post%2Dwedding%20ceremony.
45. Price, Simon. *Religions of the Ancient Greeks*.
46. https://www.spartareconsidered.com/spartan-marriage.html
47. Sophocles, *Frag. 719 (Dindorf Edition),* translation by G. E. Mylonas, *Eleusis and the Eleusinian Mysteries*. p 284
48. https://www.hellenion.org/dionysos/blessed-blessed/
49. Note that an oracle is called a Pythia, rather than that being the name of one person.
50. https://www.metmuseum.org/perspectives/articles/2021/7/ancient-greek-olympic-games#:~:text=The%20ancient%20games%20featured%20many,five%20events)%2C%20and%20boxing.
51. https://carlos.emory.edu/sites/default/files/2021-08/RA%20Religion%20and%20Ritual.pdf

52. https://www.worldhistory.org/article/833/the-athenian-calendar/
53. Parke, H.W. *Festivals of the Athenians.*
54. https://www.hellenic.org.au/post/the-thesmophoria-women-s-ritual-in-the-ancient-world
55. https://www.hellenicgods.org/theurgy---thaeouryia---theourgia
56. Davies, Owen. *Magic: A Very Short Introduction.* Oxford: Oxford University Press. 2012.
57. Parker, Robert. *Polytheism and Society at Athens.* Oxford University Press. 2005.
58. https://hellenicfaith.com/prayer-format/
59. https://www.tertullian.org/fathers/julian_apostate_2_mother.htm
60. https://blogs.bl.uk/digitisedmanuscripts/2021/02/love-spells.html
61. https://www.hellenic.org.au/post/the-allure-of-curses-and-magic-in-ancient-greece
62. Luck, Georg. *Arcana Mundi.*
63. Farone, Christopher A. *Binding and Burying the Forces of Evil: The Defensive Use of "Voodoo Dolls" in Ancient Greece Author(s).* University of California Press. 1991.
64. https://www.worldhistory.org/article/926/magic-in-ancient-greece/
65. https://classicalpolytheism.wordpress.com/2018/08/17/prayers-of-ancient-greece/
66. A statesman from Athens.
67. https://www.merriam-webster.com/dictionary/primordial#:~:text=primordial%20%E2%80%A2%20%5Cprye%2DMOR%2D,or%20organ%202%20%3A%20fundamental%2C%20primary
68. Note – I did not include all of Apollo's potential lovers, as there are many.
69. Hooper, Linda Rosewood. *Artemis and Orion.* UCSU, 2002.

70. https://www.gutenberg.org/files/21765/21765-h/21765-h.htm#bookVI
71. Daughter of the King of Thebes, Cadmus.
72. https://mythopedia.com/topics/hestia
73. Battle between the gods and Giants.
74. A daemon is considered a lesser spirit or deity in Greek practice, helping expand the range of influence of the gods, as well as provide further nuance into the pantheon.
75. Nymphs are female spirits connected to nature and often bound to a particular piece of land.
76. A staff or spear tipped with a pinecone-shaped end.
77. https://www.theoi.com/greek-mythology/personifications.html
78. https://www.theoi.com/greek-mythology/personifications.html
79. Naiads were nymphs of freshwater: springs, fountains, streams, rivers, and lakes.
80. https://www.gutenberg.org/files/3160/3160-h/3160-h.htm

Bibliography

https://chs.harvard.edu/

https://en.wikipedia.org/wiki/Greek_mythology

https://hellenicfaith.com/

https://www.hellenic.org.au/

https://www.hellenicgods.org/

https://olympioi.com/

https://www.theoi.com

Alwang, Camryn. *Marriage and Abduction Myths of the Ancient Greeks: A Means of Reinforcing the Patriarchy*. Honors Thesis. SUNY New Palz. 2021.

Amos, H.D. and A.G.P. Lang. *These Were the Greeks*. Dufour Editions, Inc. 1979.

Athanassakis, Apostolos N. and Benjamin M. Wolkow. *The Orphic Hymns*. Johns Hopkins University Press. 2013.

Budin, Stephanie Lynn. *The Ancient Greeks: An Introduction*. Oxford University Press. 2004.

Burkert, Walter. *Greek Religion*. Basil Blackwell Publisher and Harvard University Press.1985.

Buxton, Richard. *The Complete World of Greek Mythology*. Thames & Hudson. 2004.

Dieter Betz, Hans, Editor. *The Greek Magical Papyri in Translation*. The University of Chicago Press. 1986.

Fantham, Elaine, Helene Peet Foley, Natalie Noymel Kampen, Sarah B. Pomeroy, and H. Alan Shapiro. Women in the Classical World. Oxford University Press. 1994.

Farone, Christopher A. *Binding and Burying the Forces of Evil: The Defensive Use of "Voodoo Dolls" in Ancient Greece*. University of California Press. 1991.

Garland, Robert. *Daily Life of the Ancient Greeks*. Second Edition. Hackett Publishing Company. 2008.

Graziosi, Barbara. *The Gods of Olympus: A History*. Metropolitan Books. 2014.

Hamilton, Edith. *Mythology*. Little, Brown and Company. 1942.

Hatab, Lawrence J. *Myth and Philosophy: A Contest of Truths*. Open Court Publishing Company. 1990.

Hesiod. *Theogony*. Translated by M.L. West. Oxford University Press. 1988.

Hesiod. *Works and Days*. Translated by Dorothea Wender. Penguin Classics. 1976.

Homer. *The Iliad*. Translated by Caroline Alexander. HarperCollins Publishers. 2015.

Homer. *The Iliad*. Translated by Emily Wilson. W.W. Norton & Company. 2023.

Homer. *The Odyssey*. Translated by Alexander Pope. Digireads.com. 2016.

Homer. *The Odyssey*. Translated by Emily Wilson. W.W. Norton & Company. 2017.

The Hymns of Orpheus. Translated by Thomas Taylor from Ancient Greek. Preliminary Dissertation. 1792.

Koutsopetrou, Sotiria. *Rape and Rape Culture in the Ancient Greek Culture? Was rape 'really' rape in Ancient Greece?* Master's Thesis. University of Bergen. 2019.

Luck, Georg. *Arcana Mundi: Magic and the Occult in the Greek and Roman Worlds*. The Johns Hopkins University Press. 1985.

Morris, Ian. *Death-Ritual and Social Structure in Classical Antiquity*. Cambridge University Press. 1992.

Morris, Ian and Barry B. Powell. *The Greeks: History, Culture, and Society*. Pearson Prentice Hall. 2006.

Parke, H.W. *Festivals of the Athenians*. Thames and Hudson: London, 1977.

Price, Simon. *Religions of the Ancient Greeks*. Cambridge University Press. 1999.

Sansone, David. *Ancient Greek Civilization*. Blackwell Publishing. 2017.

Sophocles, Frag. 719 (Dindorf edition), *Eleusis and the Eleusinian Mysteries*. Translated by G. E. Mylonas. Princeton: Princeton University Press, 1961.

Tsantsanoglou, Kyriakos. *The Derveni Papyrus: An Interdisciplinary Research Project*. The Center for Hellenic Studies. 2006.

Zaidman, Louise Bruit, Pauline Schmitt Pantel, and Paul Cartledge. *Religion in the Ancient Greek City*. Cambridge University Press. 1989.

About the Author

Irisanya Moon (she/they) is a priestess, teacher, and initiate in the Reclaiming tradition. She has taught classes and camps around the world, including in the US, Canada, UK, and Australia. Irisanya writes a Substack newsletter called Heart Magick, which can be found at https://irisanya.substack.com/

You can find out more about Irisanya's writing and teaching at... www.irisanyamoon.com

Books by Irisanya Moon...

Earth Spirit

Gaia: Saving Her, Saving Ourselves

Honoring the Wild: Reclaiming Witchcraft & Environmental Activism

Pagan Portals

Reclaiming Witchcraft

Aphrodite – Encountering the Goddess of Love & Beauty & Initiation

Iris – Goddess of the Rainbow and Messenger of the Godds

The Norns – Weavers of Fate and Magick

Artemis – Goddess of the Wild Hunt & Sovereign Heart

Circe – Goddess of Sorcery

Hestia – Goddess of Hearth, Home & Community

Practically Pagan

An Alternative Guide to Health & Well-being

Other Books in the *Pantheon* Series

The Egyptians
Robin Herne
978-1-78535-504-2 (Paperback)
978-1-78535-505-9 (e-book)

The Greeks
Irisanya Moon
978-1-78535-506-6 (Paperback)
978-1-78535-507-3 (e-book)

The Minoans
Laura Perry
978-1-80341-627-4 (Paperback)
978-1-80341-914-5 (e-book)

The Norse
Morgan Daimler
978-1-78904-141-5 (Paperback)
978-1-78904-142-2 (e-book)

The Romans
Rachel Roberts
978-1-80341-682-3 (Paperback)
978-1-80341-930-5 (e-book)

The Welsh
Mhara Starling
978-1-80341-742-4 (Paperback)
978-1-80341-741-7 (e-book)

MOON BOOKS

PAGANISM & SHAMANISM

What is Paganism? A religion, a spirituality, an alternative belief system, nature worship? You can find support for all these definitions (and many more) in dictionaries, encyclopaedias, and text books of religion, but subscribe to any one and the truth will evade you. Above all Paganism is a creative pursuit, an encounter with reality, an exploration of meaning and an expression of the soul. Druids, Heathens, Wiccans and others, all contribute their insights and literary riches to the Pagan tradition. Moon Books invites you to begin or to deepen your own encounter, right here, right now.

If you have enjoyed this book, why not tell other readers by posting a review on your preferred book site.

Bestsellers from Moon Books

Keeping Her Keys

An Introduction to Hekate's Modern Witchcraft

Cyndi Brannen

Blending Hekate, witchcraft and personal development together to create a powerful new magickal perspective.

Paperback: 978-1-78904-075-3 ebook 978-1-78904-076-0

Journey to the Dark Goddess

How to Return to Your Soul

Jane Meredith

Discover the powerful secrets of the Dark Goddess and transform your depression, grief and pain into healing and integration.

Paperback: 978-1-84694-677-6 ebook: 978-1-78099-223-5

Shamanic Reiki

Expanded Ways of Working with Universal Life Force Energy

Llyn Roberts, Robert Levy

Shamanism and Reiki are each powerful ways of healing; together, their power multiplies. Shamanic Reiki introduces techniques to help healers and Reiki practitioners tap ancient healing wisdom.

Paperback: 978-1-84694-037-8 ebook: 978-1-84694-650-9

Southern Cunning

Folkloric Witchcraft in the American South

Aaron Oberon

Modern witchcraft with a Southern flair, this book is a journey through the folklore of the American South and a look at the power these stories hold for modern witches.

Paperback: 978-1-78904-196-5 ebook: 978-1-78904-197-2

Bestsellers from Moon Books

Pagan Portals Series

The Morrigan

Meeting the Great Queens

Morgan Daimler

Ancient and enigmatic, the Morrigan reaches out to us. On shadowed wings and in raven's call, meet the ancient Irish goddess of war, battle, prophecy, death, sovereignty, and magic.

Paperback: 978-1-78279-833-0 ebook: 978-1-78279-834-7

The Awen Alone

Walking the Path of the Solitary Druid

Joanna van der Hoeven

An introductory guide for the solitary Druid, The Awen Alone will accompany you as you explore, and seek out your own place within the natural world.

Paperback: 978-1-78279-547-6 ebook: 978-1-78279-546-9

Moon Magic

Rachel Patterson

An introduction to working with the phases of the Moon, what they are and how to live in harmony with the lunar year and to utilise all the magical powers it provides.

Paperback: 978-1-78279-281-9 ebook: 978-1-78279-282-6

Hekate

A Devotional

Vivienne Moss

Hekate, Queen of Witches and the Shadow-Lands, haunts the pages of this devotional bringing magic and enchantment into your lives.

Paperback: 978-1-78535-161-7 ebook: 978-1-78535-162-4

Readers of ebooks can buy or view any of these bestsellers by clicking on the live link in the title. Most titles are published in paperback and as an ebook. Paperbacks are available in traditional bookshops. Both print and ebook formats are available online.

Find more titles and sign up to our readers' newsletter
www.collectiveinkbooks.com/paganism

For video content, author interviews and more, please subscribe to our YouTube channel.

MoonBooksPublishing

Follow us on social media for book news, promotions and more:

Facebook: Moon Books

Instagram: @MoonBooksCI

X: @MoonBooksCI

TikTok: @MoonBooksCI